WALKING
WITH
HENRI NOUWEN

Also by Robert Waldron
published by Paulist Press

Walking with Thomas Merton

WALKING WITH HENRI NOUWEN

A Reflective Journey

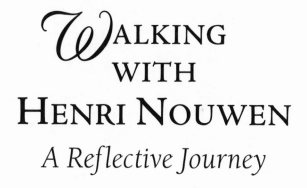

Robert Waldron

Paulist Press
New York/ Mahwah, N.J.

PERMISSIONS AND ACKNOWLEDGMENTS:

Excerpts from *Love Had a Compass: Journals and Poetry* by Robert Lax, copyright © 1996 by Robert Lax. Used by permission of Grove/Atlantic.

Excerpts from *Genesee Diary* by Henri J.M. Nouwen, copyright © 1976 by Henri J.M. Nouwen. Used by permission of Doubleday, a division of Random House, Inc.

Excerpts from *The Sabbatical Journey: The Diary of His Final Year* by Henri J.M. Nouwen, copyright © 1998 by Henri J.M. Nouwen. Used by permission of Crossroad Publishing, 1998.

Excerpts from *The Collected Poetry of Wallace Stevens* by Wallace Stevens, copyright © 1999 by Wallace Stevens. Used by permission of Alfred A. Knopf.

Unless otherwise noted, scripture extracts are taken from the New Revised Standard Version, Copyright © 1989, by the Division of Christian Education of the National Council of the Churches of Christ in the United States of America and reprinted by permission of the publisher.

Cover design by Sharyn Banks
Book design by Lynn Else

Library of Congress Cataloging-in-Publication Data
Waldron, Robert.
    Walking with Henri Nouwen : a reflective journey / Robert Waldron.
        p. cm.
    Includes bibliographical references.
    ISBN 0-8091-4161-2 (alk. paper)
    1. Nouwen, Henri J. M. I Title.
    BX4705.N87 W35 2003
    282'.092—dc21

                                                                    2003011214

Published by Paulist Press
997 Macarthur Boulevard
Mahwah, New Jersey 07430

www.paulistpress.com

Printed and bound in the United States of America

Contents

❧ ❧

Dedicated to the memory of my uncle
Robert F. Flynn

Preface

❧ ❧

When I set forth on my trip to Washington, D.C., the media had focused their attention on the Vermeer Exhibit at the National Gallery. Few people knew about the Winslow Homer Exhibit simultaneously presented by the National Gallery. With only twenty-one paintings, Vermeer was the superstar with top billing and international coverage. For most of the morning, I was enthralled by the Dutch painter who reminds us of the beautiful in the dailiness of life. I spent a brief time with Homer because I knew the exhibit would soon make its way to my home city, Boston.

A stone's throw from the White House is the Renwick Gallery on Pennsylvania Avenue. On my way back to Georgetown, I decided to drop in since I'd never before visited this museum, but my real motive, I must admit, was to find respite from the sleet and snow that had transformed December 12 into a blustery winter day.

The gallery on the first floor housed *Rick Dillingham: A Retrospective Exhibit.* I knew nothing about the artist and practically nothing about his art of pottery-making. Beautiful pottery of globes, cones, cylinders, disks, and gas cans caught my eye. Molded and glazed to perfection, they glowed with intriguing geometric, abstract designs and variegated colors of burnished gold, silver, and ebony. Never an aficionado of pottery, I was both enchanted and baffled by this art form that was remarkably different from all other pottery I had seen.

Dillingham is an artist of brinkmanship: he deliberately shatters his bisque-fired pot into pieces, paints each shard, a miniature canvas unto itself, and reconstructs the pot for refirement, allowing the mend marks to be visible. The reassembled pottery represents a new, transformed beauty that boldly declares its previous brokenness. In fact, its brokenness renders Dillingham's creations more beautiful and unique. This is minimalism turned upside down, illustrating not so much that less is more but that the whole is more than the sum of its parts.

The idea of taking what was broken, what many would consider useless, and transforming it into something more lovely haunted me on my return airplane trip to Boston. The poet Edward A. Robinson says that "most things break," including people. We all break down at some point in our lives either with physical or psychic illness. This is a fact of life. But great things can emerge from such breakage. I think of the poet Theodore Roethke who suffered a nervous breakdown but on recovery said, "That wasn't a breakdown but a break-up!" because he became a saner and more whole person, perhaps even a greater poet. Ignatius Loyola founded the Society of Jesus after an illness and a spiritual crisis. John of the Cross wrote his greatest poetry while in prison, as monks of his order tried to break his spirit. The poet Francis Thompson, broken by addiction to opium, emerged from his dark night to compose his luminous spiritual autobiography, *The Hound of Heaven*. T. S. Eliot emerged from his brokenness chronicled in *The Waste Land* to write his spiritual masterpiece of faith, *The Four Quartets*. C. S. Lewis left behind his atheism and loneliness to write *Surprised by Joy*. Dorothy Day, out of her brokenness, converted to Catholicism and founded the Catholic Worker movement and later wrote *The Long Loneliness*.

Dillingham's pottery is an exhortation not to give up, not to despair. His small, unheralded exhibit reminded me of things I had forgotten, things I needed to remember, even in my teaching. My students and I were studying Shakespeare's *King Lear*. In his egotism Lear commands his three daughters to inform him how much each of them loves him. Goneril and Regan are unctuous in their flattery, and Lear apportions his kingdom accordingly. He reserves the largest and richest portion of his domain for his favorite daughter, Cordelia. When her time comes to express her love, she says, "Nothing, my lord." Lear rejoins, "Nothing will come of nothing." (1.1.99). When I inform my students that this line is the heart of the play, they look at me perplexed. And now after viewing Dillingham's art, I believe I have come to a deeper understanding of how blind Lear is to say "Nothing will come of nothing." Stripped of ego, power, soldiers, friends, kingdom, Lear is reduced to nothing. At zero point, King Lear breaks into being a whole person capable of compassion as he shifts his self-mesmerized gaze from the "I" onto Others. For the first time in his life, he empathizes with the suffering of his fellow men and women:

> Poor naked wretches, whereso'er you are,
> That bide the pelting of this pitiless storm,
> How shall your houseless heads and unfed sides,

> Your looped and windowed raggedness, defend you
> From seasons such as these? O, I have ta'en
> Too little care of this! Take physic, pomp;
> Expose thyself to feel what wretches feel,
> That thou mays't shake the superflux to them
> And show the heavens more just. (3.4. 35–43)

The naked, the homeless—to these Lear had never given a thought. And never would have had he not been broken: himself naked, homeless, friendless, and hungry. Broken by misfortune, a king finally becomes a whole person.

That we are all broken by sin is knowledge all Christians understand. To transform our brokenness, Christ came on earth. He subjected himself to the breaking of the crucifixion only to rise again on the third day. Of course, in a public school, I'm not allowed to speak of Christ or the New Testament. But I can point out to my students that King Lear is broken by selfishness and a lack of self-knowledge. "He hath ever but slenderly known himself," says one of his daughters. Lear creates most of his problems by his own brokenness, which he refuses to acknowledge. The humility of self-knowledge could have prevented much pain and suffering. But suffering is the kiln through which we all must eventually pass. Malcolm Muggeridge once said that he never learned much about life or himself when things went his way; only through suffering did he learn life's most valuable lessons.

My favorite parable is the Prodigal Son, which I also see differently now; it illustrates the theme of brokenness transformed into beauty. The younger son takes his inheritance, squandering it in a life of dissipation until he is a homeless and broken man. While feeding the pigs, he realizes that his life is shattered. He decides to return home. His father sees him from a distance and runs to him. No questions asked. Forgiveness given unconditionally. His father orders his servants to clothe him in the finest robe, to adorn his hand with a ring, to shod his feet in sandals, and to kill the fatted calf for a feast to celebrate the return of his lost son. The father transforms his broken son by the beauty of love symbolized by the new, fine clothes, ring, and feast. What is lost is found again; what is broken is whole again.

We are all God's prodigal children. We have the potential to transform our brokenness into something quite beautiful simply by returning home to the Father. No vociferous mea culpa is necessary. The father sped to his son before he heard one word of contrition.

And now I come to Henri Nouwen. Of all the spiritual writers I have read in my life, no one understands brokenness so acutely, compassionately, and wisely. He deeply delved into his own woundedness, so profoundly that he could subsequently refer to himself as a "wounded healer." By walking with Nouwen, I've come to understand his wounding and how he transcended it. He is a model for all of us when he says that our wounds are our greatest gift. If we accept them in the right spirit, they break us into beauty.

Walking with Henri Nouwen

～〜

Summertime again. I've decided to follow the plan I used last summer and keep a journal. I'm spending the summer with Henri Nouwen because I've chosen the fall of 2001 for my first Thomas Merton/Nouwen Retreat. Without doubt these two men are the most famous spiritual writers of the latter part of the twentieth century. I've been reading them most of my adult life although I came first to Merton in high school when I read *The Seven Storey Mountain*. Nouwen came later when I purchased a little paperback, *Pray to Live: Thomas Merton: Contemplative Critic*, which addressed the life and thought of the man I had up until then most admired. I enjoyed reading Nouwen's book: he wrote simply and beautifully about Merton's monastic life and carefully excerpted from Merton's published works pivotal passages about the contemplative life. And I could see that he himself was a deeply spiritual man.

Where does one start with Nouwen? He's written more than forty books, nearly as prolific as Merton. Perhaps I'll begin with my favorite, *Genesee Diary*.

Weather in the 90s and uncomfortably humid.

During most of his life, Nouwen hungered for attention. His international fame was surprisingly never enough. His mother raised him according to a child-rearing theory of a German doctor who believed the grasping/egotistical nature of children could be controlled by restricting their intake of food and physical touch. Henri ended up being a touched-deprived child—an impoverishment that haunted him for the rest of his life.[1]

Merton suffered in a similar fashion. His mother, Ruth Jenkins Merton, raised him according to the book. She attentively watched her son grow and recorded everything about him: appetite, physical growth, speech, intellectual development, and so forth, in what she called "Tom's Book." She was stinting in her expression of love and affection. In his autobiography he said "perhaps solitaries are made by severe mothers."[2]

As adults, both men felt homeless. Merton finally found his home in the Cistercian order. Nouwen's search was longer and more agonizing. For a time he thought academia would suit him, but they were cerebrally cold places: Notre Dame, Yale, and Harvard. He eventually found a home among the mentally handicapped of Daybreak, Toronto.

When Jean Vanier invited him to L'Arche in Trosly, France, a home for the handicapped, Nouwen accepted. Later, he received a letter that would change his life forever, a letter from Daybreak in Toronto. Joe Egan writes:

> This letter comes to you from the Daybreak Community Council and we are asking you to consider coming to live with us in our community of Daybreak....We truly feel that you have a gift to bring us. At the same

time, our sense is that Daybreak would be a good place for you, too. We would want to support you in your important vocation of writing and speaking by providing you with a home and with a community that will love you and call you to grow.[3]

I suspect that Nouwen's heart skipped a beat when he read, "by providing you with a home." It was at Daybreak that he was assigned to care for a young man by the name of Adam. It was perhaps the most liberating and life-enhancing experience of his life.

Both men were diarists. I've always been attracted to the diary genre: it is an intimate format, and one has a better opportunity to get to know the writer. Merton's journals are now all published, but I'm not certain if this is true of Nouwen. Merton's diaries tend to record his intellectual interests whereas Nouwen records his daily emotional and spiritual struggles. Whereas Merton never completely reveals himself, Nouwen stands nude before his readers; thus, we see him in his complete vulnerability. Nouwen is willing to take such a risk knowing full well that appearing so nakedly before his readers he might alienate them with such an honest record of his frailties. However, the amazing result is that the opposite happens: the reader sees himself in Nouwen who becomes a mirror for all of us Christians who daily fail to be "perfect as your heavenly Father is perfect."

Both Nouwen and Merton were attracted to Rainer Maria Rilke. Nouwen went to Rilke because he "will help me to see."[4] Nouwen especially admired Rilke's letters to his wife Clara about

Cezanne's paintings. Cezanne was a painter, Nouwen says, who was "present to the present"[5]—I love that phrase. I also want to deliberately live in the present so that, like Thoreau, when I come to the end of my life, I won't look back to find that I've sleep-walked through my life.

Merton went to Rilke because as a poet he was attracted to Rilke's verse-making and his talent for losing himself in the contemplative experience.

When Rilke worked for Rodin, the great sculptor advised Rilke to visit the zoo and to watch the animals closely. Only then would he understand what sculpting was all about. Not until one achieves an "inseeing" does one know what goes into the creative experience. By "inseeing," Rilke meant an intense identification with the object of our gazing to the point that our inseeing becomes an outseeing: the ego disappears.

The temporary disappearance of the ego seems to be the key not only of the aesthetic but also of the spiritual experience.

There is a tape of Merton teaching Rilke to the novices of Gethsemani. His joy about Rilke comes through. He reads to them one of his favorite Rilke poems, "The Panther":

> His gaze those bars keep passing is so misted
> with tiredness, it can take in nothing more.
> He feels as though a thousand bars existed,
> and no more world beyond them than before.
>
> Those supply-powerful paddings, turning there
> in tiniest of circles, well might be

the dance of forces round a centre where
some mighty will stands paralyticly.

Just now and then the pupil's noiseless shutter
is lifted—Then an image will indart,
down through the limb's intensive stillness flutter,
and ends its being in the heart.[6]

Merton believed along with his favorite English poet, William
Blake, that the spiritual life is a matter of "cleansing the doors of
perception" so that we can see. But seeing must penetrate through
what is false in order to find the true. Perhaps our prayer shouldn't
be "Lord, help my unbelief" but "Lord, help my unseeing."

I used to frequent the St. Thomas More bookstore in Harvard
Square. One day I saw Nouwen, whom I had recently heard
preach at St. Paul's Church in Cambridge, but I was too shy to
introduce myself. I wish I had. In my mind's eye, I still see him
wearing a scarf, beret, and tweed jacket, sitting in a chair quietly
observing the customers.

As a child Nouwen's play centered around his pretending to be
a priest. His grandmother condoned the game by having vest-
ments designed for him and an altar constructed. It is now said
that Nouwen had always wanted to be a priest.

I wonder if perhaps there's something not quite right about
encouraging Nouwen's youthful identification with the priesthood. It smacks of psychological conditioning. Had he been pro-
grammed by his family to want to be a priest and nothing else

from his early childhood? Had he on some level understood that this would make his mother and grandparents happy? Perhaps he was a precociously pious child, and I should leave it at that. But because he suffered from poor self-esteem and depression most of his life, I cannot help wondering about the source of his vocation.

I cannot banish from my mind's eye a grown-up Nouwen weeping uncontrollably; the only way to comfort him was for his therapists to physically embrace him until his weeping ceased, and he was calmed.

It's ironic that his first book's title was *Intimacy: Essays in Pastoral Psychology*—intimacy was the very thing for which he hungered.

I'm not surprised that Nouwen was attracted to psychology. Psychology is a science that was not popular with Catholics of the 1960s. Nouwen was likely drawn to it because he was aware of his own neuroses. He was a man who wanted to know himself in order to help others.

Michael Ford's biography, *Wounded Prophet*, frankly addresses Nouwen's homosexuality. What does a priest do who believes he is a homosexual? Does he accept himself? Hate himself? Administer to himself?

And what can the church do for him?

Nouwen's mother taught him the prayer he based his life upon: "All for you, dear Jesus."

Frightening thunderstorms today. Scared my new puppy. Scared me! Now it's back to hot and humid weather. Where are the sunny, dry, delightful days of past Junes? Seems we have fewer and fewer springlike days. Global warming be damned.

On Sunday, July 21, 1957, Nouwen was ordained a priest. On that day I was ten years old and at camp in New Hampshire, and I had just celebrated my tenth birthday on July 20.

For an ordination gift his Uncle Anton, also a priest, gave his nephew Henri a chalice, the very one Anton had received from Henri's grandmother; it was adorned with his grandmother's diamonds.

Important dates in Nouwen's life:

1932—Born in Holland
1957—Ordained a Roman Catholic priest in the
    Diocese of Utrecht
1964–66—Studied psychology at the Menninger
    Foundation in the United States
1968–70—Returned to the Netherlands to teach
1971–81—Professor of pastoral theology at Yale University
1983–85—Professor and lecturer at Harvard
1986–96—Pastor of L'Arche Daybreak in Toronto
September 21, 1996—Nouwen died of a heart attack in the Netherlands while en route to St. Petersburg for the making of a documentary about Rembrandt's famous painting, *The Return of the Prodigal Son*, housed at the Hermitage.

Nouwen stayed at the Trappist Abbey of Genesee in upstate New York for seven months starting in June 1974. He went there to face his restlessness. Nouwen wasn't there many days before he started dreaming of Thomas Merton. Merton was Nouwen's ideal: the *contemplative writer*. That in a nutshell is what Nouwen aspired to be. For Nouwen, Merton was the paragon to be emulated; thus the experiment of living as a Trappist.

I'm glad Nouwen went to Genesee for two reasons: first, he wrote one of the best diaries about the spiritual life; second, he became friends with Abbot John Eudes Bamberger who knew Thomas Merton as a student, brother monk, and advisor. This friendship would mean a lot to Nouwen although he and John Eudes disagreed on several issues.

John Eudes was good for Nouwen because he was a no-nonsense kind of guy who didn't mince his words. Nouwen was a charismatic speaker and people would more often than not end up adoring him, rendering them less likely to tell him the truth, and he too much relished their praise. John Eudes would give him down-to-earth advice to ponder. Bamberger says, "Fr. Henri, during his stay at the Abbey of Genesee, gave serious consideration to entering the monastery. However, when it was pointed out to him that he was suited rather to a ministry that included a large involvement in teaching, preaching and spiritual direction, and that he required the stimulus of on-going contacts with a variety of people, he soon perceived the truth of this view."[7]

In one entry Nouwen says, "the only reason I should be here [Genesee] is to learn how to pray." A remarkable admission by a priest of seventeen years.[8]

Merton was the son of artists. He describes his father Owen Merton as an artist who painted like Cezanne. Merton himself had a painter's eye. But Nouwen was an aficionado of art, often moved by painting to the point of life-transformation. For instance, Nouwen loved Rembrandt's *The Return of the Prodigal Son*, and he greatly admired the work of Vincent Van Gogh whom he portrayed in a small one-man play. Both artists helped him move through his psychological depressions.

Last Lent I conducted a reading group for the Pauline Bookstore. One of the books chosen for discussion was Nouwen's meditations on Rembrandt's *The Return of the Prodigal Son*. It's a handsome book with Rembrandt's painting on the cover and another copy included on the inside for meditation. The nuns who run the store made a huge poster of the painting and placed it before our semicircle of chairs so that during the whole discussion we could gaze upon this beautiful portrait.

Readers were moved by Nouwen's interpretation of the parable as one of unconditional love. We read aloud the parable, and they were particularly moved by the father's running to his lost son, embracing him on the spot, and then calling for a party and for his son to be decked with fine clothes and jewelry. One reader said, "His father asked for no apology." No, I remarked, unconditional love needs none.

This parable meant much to Nouwen because his own relationship with his father was strained. His mother was delighted that her son wanted to be a priest; his father, however, was more worldly and said to him, "Show me that you can accomplish something."[9]

I must try to understand more deeply why "The Return of the Prodigal Son" parable meant so much to Nouwen. On the face of it, Nouwen wasn't a son who wasted his inheritance. He was not a profligate who ended up feeding the pigs. On the contrary, he had a distinguished career at some of the world's most respected universities and wrote a number of best-selling books, some of which have become spiritual classics. Then why did he feel like the son who had greatly failed? Or was his sense of unworthiness related to his homosexuality?

Nouwen's delight in Rembrandt's portrait of the Prodigal Son led him to study the life of the artist who, I gather, led a rather hedonistic life as a young man. Rembrandt's lust for women, money, and fame led to his losing everything; in addition, there were the deaths of several of his children, including his favorite son Titus. By the end of his life, he was so poor he had to auction off all his possessions and lived his remaining days with his daughter Cornelia.

Nouwen believes that what Rembrandt lost in wealth, he gained in the wisdom evident in his last paintings. The artist's suffering and disillusionment purified him to the point that he developed the "penetrating eye," the eye that sees beyond the superficial.[10]

Shakespeare was 42 years old when Rembrandt was born in 1606. Oh, how gloriously Rembrandt would have painted King Lear who at the end of his life had only his daughter Cordelia by his side. Similarly, Rembrandt had his daughter Cornelia.

Two men who lost everything only to discover what mattered most: love.

I'm much intrigued by Nouwen's reference to Rembrandt developing the "penetrating eye." I've been thinking about it all afternoon. There is no magical mirror into which we can gaze to determine the state of our soul. We must depend upon our own willingness to develop the penetrating eye that sees through the many masks we've devised, as well as the bad habits, illusions, and delusions by which we live.

The penetrating eye sees beyond all that is false, through all that obscures our True Self. Developing the penetrating eye demands huge effort and utter honesty. Few are up to it. It's so difficult that T. S. Eliot once wrote that "humankind cannot bear much reality."[11]

Nouwen suggests that Jesus is also a Prodigal Son who must lose everything in order to go out in search of all other prodigal sons (and daughters). Nouwen also believes that the father figure in Rembrandt's painting is nearly blind. Wonder why he thinks this? I think it unlikely because the father couldn't have seen his son from a distance.[12]

Or had Nouwen meant that he is blind to his son's sins?

I re-read the parable of the Prodigal Son in Luke (Luke 15:11–23). "While he was still far away his father saw him and took pity, and he ran and fell upon his neck and kissed him repeatedly." First of all, his father's eyesight had surely not diminished for he saw his son "while he was still far away." Was he always on the lookout for him? Or was he simply an extremely attentive man?

Although an old man, the father was in good physical shape for he ran to his son. And then the most touching part of the story: he repeatedly kissed his son. How many kisses before he gave his son a chance to say anything? The father uttered not a single, "I told you so." He spoke only love, acceptance, and joy at his son's return.

At Yale (1971–81), Nouwen wrote twelve books. Like Merton, Nouwen was a born writer. Even at the end of his life, Nouwen was still honing his craft. He wanted to branch out to other kinds of writing. I suspect he wanted to be a novelist.

Nouwen's stay at Genesee was time well spent. He had to see with his own eyes that as beautiful as it is, the monastic life wasn't his vocation. I well understand his ambivalence: to be drawn simultaneously to the solitary life and its peace, prayer, and canonical structure and also to the world with its people, energy, and activities. Because he wanted both, he'd have to learn to be a monk in the world. Which is exactly what he did become, but it's unlikely he'd ever describe himself in such a manner, that is, a worldly monk.

Merton also suffered from a similar ambivalence. He loved his solitude, but like Nouwen he was greatly drawn to people. He was paradoxically a hermit and a joiner, a loner and people lover. The biggest difference between Merton and Nouwen is, I believe, that Nouwen *desperately* needed the approval of others. Without his daily dose of affirmation, Nouwen could easily fall into crippling depression. As far as I know, Merton didn't need others in such a fashion.

Nouwen was moved by Merton's Louisville Vision. He records in his diary a similar epiphany:

> When I walked into a flower shop to buy some white and yellow chrysanthemums for friends in town I felt a deep love for the florist who, with a twinkle in his eye, told me that chrysanthemums were "year-round flowers," not bound to the seasons. I felt open, free, and relaxed and really enjoyed the little conversation we had on flowers, presidents, and honesty in politics.[13]

Nouwen credited solitude with his increased sensitivity to the good in people.

Today is a delicious summer day of cool, dry air. It's amazing to me how humidity can drag one down. On hot and humid days I can barely move myself from my chair. Today I'm filled with energy, so much so I take my puppy at 5:30 a.m. to the park where he runs around me in circles.

One way to be sure to see the sunrise is to have a puppy-in-training.

I went to Victor Hugo's bookstore on Newbury Street in Boston. An amazing coincidence: from the over 100,000 used books, I took down two books from the shelves; both showed the signatures of former owners and I knew both!

I made my way to Sheehan's, a Catholic bookstore that also sells used books. It had a good collection of Nouwen volumes, and I purchased one I didn't have, *Making All Things New: An Invitation to the Spiritual Life*; it's one of the last books he wrote while at Yale. I like the brief format and what he has to say about living the inner life that cannot be fostered, Nouwen insists, if we allow our lives to be dominated by worry.

Worry: how I've been plagued by worry too much of my life. All wasted time for most of the things I worried about never happened. Worry is the plague of people who want control. Christ enjoins us not to worry, "Do not worry" (Matt 6:25). Three little words: so hard to follow!

What becomes quickly obvious in *Genesee Diary* is that Nouwen was a klutz. While boiling water, he burns his thumb; carrying rocks, he drops them; on the bread-line, he couldn't keep up with the bread-flow.

In a dream about Merton, Henri sees Merton dressed in brown trousers, tennis shoes, and a yellow tee shirt, sandpapering and painting a bench. Nouwen asks him questions about nails and screws, but Merton remains silent in a friendly fashion and seems to be saying "be quiet and watch and learn."[14]

Interpretation of dream: Henri wishes he were more practical, more relaxed, more silent. Merton is his ideal man, one who knows how to live in a pragmatic and spiritual way. Merton integrates both *ora et labora* (prayer and work) in his life. Perhaps that's the integration Nouwen is looking for at Genesee.

It's amusing that Henri considers making his own lunch at Genesee to be "fun." He strikes me as the stereotypical absent-minded professor. Certainly his privileged upper class background comes through. Luckily, during much of his life, Nouwen had many practical friends who were willing to do things for him: from typing his manuscripts to washing his clothes to cooking his meals. Later, he became a star on the spiritual circuit and a bestselling author to boot. Then came the increasing fame—a blessing and a curse, for both Nouwen and Merton.

It would perhaps be unkind to say Nouwen was spoiled. Although it's likely he was. But he observed this in himself and tried to address it. A man as honestly introspective as Nouwen knew his character flaws—which is good. What isn't good is that he couldn't forgive his imperfections. He never completely learned how to relax into just being Henri Nouwen. That is a significant difference between Merton and Nouwen: Merton eventually enjoyed being himself, although it took him many years to learn to accept himself, warts and all. Nouwen seemingly remained conflicted even up to his death—all quite evident in his last diary. But one can be conflicted and still have peace of mind. I believe that Henri finally surrendered his divided self to God.

Merton was also a klutz. The danger of being a spiritual man is that one often becomes clumsy and awkward in the world. If you keep your gaze on eternity, you lose contact with Mother Earth, and she has ways of letting you know she doesn't like to be ignored. Don't pay attention to your boiling water, she'll burn your finger. Don't pay attention to moving rocks and boulders, she'll drop one on your toe. Don't watch the bread, you'll be inundated with dough. The spiritual way is not so terribly different from the practical way: both demand ATTENTION.

Simone Weil says that absolute attention is prayer.

I'm re-reading BBC producer Michael Ford's biography *Wounded Prophet: A Portrait of Henri J. M. Nouwen*. It's a good biography—frank about the many problems of loneliness, anxiety, and insecurity Father Nouwen faced. Ford is not afraid to address Nouwen's sexuality, which he accomplishes in a most humane and compassionate way.

The church has yet to give us a homosexual saint. Perhaps God has given us one in Father Nouwen. He was always a priest first. And he remained faithful to his life of celibacy—probably at great psychic cost.

The only other famous Catholic writer I can think of who could also serve as a homosexual paragon is Father Gerard Manley Hopkins. He was another priest who remained faithful to his vocation, but again accomplished at great cost. One need only read his Terrible Sonnets to measure what Hopkins endured. But at his deathbed he is reported to have said, "I am so happy."

Having been involved in academics all my life, I think I understand why it turned Nouwen off. It was likely the jockeying for advancement, the sometimes cutthroat competition and rivalry, and the ever-present dissembling that one must practice to get ahead. He wanted none of it. What he wanted was to help people come closer to Christ. Paradoxically, it was the very people at Yale who most needed to hear him. Whoever said that to mention God in a college faculty room would empty it faster than to scream "Fire!" was on the mark.

Nouwen knew intuitively, I believe, that being himself was problematic at places like Yale and Harvard. If Nouwen had been the butt of many a secret joke at the Yale and Harvard campuses, all said ever so discreetly over a glass of sherry in a dark-paneled faculty lounge, I wouldn't be surprised. That's no reflection on Nouwen himself, just that religion is itself too often mocked and disparaged in our American intellectual milieu.

This is a theme I address in my new novel *Blue Hope*.

The image of Henri trying to knock a gatepost down with a sledgehammer makes me smile. A Genesee monk takes pity on him and with a tractor pulls it up in a few minutes. Another time Henri is packing bread for two hours and then sticking price tags on the bags. He finds the job tiring and frustrating because he broke his glasses and could hardly see. Poor guy![15]

Another entry moves me differently. Henri says that perhaps he has found a "home" at Genesee, which is poignant because of what it implies: a lonely man without a home. In this he reminds me of Merton.

Henri also admits to writing too many letters. Like Merton he wanted to "disappear into God" and be "alone with the Alone" without telephone, letters, visitors. But having read the whole diary, I know that such a desire would fall by the wayside. Both Merton and Nouwen needed contact with people—Nouwen even more so than Merton.

Just talked to a friend last night who is friendly with a rather famous monk/writer. Now an old man in his 80s, he is a lonely man who now wonders if his life as a monk was worth it. Today in the *Boston Globe* an article appeared about a local priest who says that marriage must be an option if we are to attract young men into the priesthood. Interesting coincidence.

More lyrical summer days with temperatures in the mid-70s. Dry as an autumn leaf.

I am riveted by Nouwen's last journal *Sabbatical Journey*. He compares his sabbatical year to a garden of flowers and weeds. He hasn't a clue about how he'll get across the *field* of the next year, simultaneously afraid and excited about the unknown. It's poignant to read about his awareness of how *addicted* he is to busyness. It's a good sign when a man is on good terms with his addictions. There are some addictions that must be conquered; others are better handled by peaceful coexistence: being too busy all the time is a good example of the latter.

Nouwen admits that of all the cities he's lived in, Toronto is the one he loves most. I'm surprised that he didn't like my city of Boston. He spent much time there, but I wonder if his hectic life at Harvard left a bad taste in his mouth. Harvard has never been a comfortable place for Catholics. I think of the late George Santayana who was unhappy during his long tenure at Harvard. As soon as he could afford it, he fled Harvard without ever looking back.

Nouwen says of Harvard:

> My decision to leave Harvard was a difficult one. For many months I was not sure if I would be following or betraying my vocation by leaving. The outer voices kept saying, "You can do so much good here. People need you!" The inner voices kept saying, "What good is it to preach the Gospel to others while losing your own soul?" Finally, I realized that my increasing inner darkness, my feelings of being rejected by some of my students, colleagues, friends, and even God, my inordinate need for affirmation and affection, and my deep sense of not belonging were clear signs that I was not following the way of God's spirit. The fruits of the spirit are not sadness, loneliness, and separation, but joy, solitude, and community.[16]

That's quite an indictment of Harvard although, of course, he doesn't put all the blame on the college. But enough. He also describes Harvard as competitive, ambitious, career-oriented.[17] Gee, it sounds like my school, which one of my colleagues recently lamented is "a school without a soul."

Nouwen's prayer life during the last year of his life was problematic: it was one of aridity and darkness. He wonders if it were not better just to abandon all efforts to get closer to God.

I think he's wise to foster abandonment at this point in life. He should hand himself over to God completely. But it would mean giving up control, and I believe Nouwen has a problem with that.

He's too goal-oriented. Having just begun his sabbatical, he's already obsessing about his new book, *Can You Drink the Cup?*

He has obviously never learned the art of relaxing.

After I wrote the above, I came across a favorite prayer of Nouwen, composed by Charles de Foucauld:

> Father,
> I abandon myself into your hands;
> do with me what you will.
> Whatever you may do, I thank you;
> I am ready for all, I accept all.
> Let only your will be done in me,
> and in all your creatures.
> I wish no more than this,
> O Lord.
>
> Into your hands I commend my soul;
> I offer it to you with all my love
> of my heart,
> for I love you, Lord,
> and so need to give myself,
> to surrender myself into your hands
> without reserve
> and with boundless confidence.
> For you are my Father.[18]

A beautiful prayer, and so unlike Nouwen's Christ-centered spirituality. In fact, he says he can't pray this prayer without "the spirit of Jesus."[19]

Nouwen says, "I want to love God, but also make a career. I want to be a good Christian, but also have my successes as a teacher, preacher or speaker. I want to be a saint, but also enjoy the sensations of a sinner."[20] He wants an awful lot. Too much ego is revealed here. I have a problem with his wanting to be a saint. Why not just be yourself, Henri Nouwen?

At the beginning of his conversion, Merton too wanted to be a saint. He finally handed that goal over to God.

Nouwen and I agree on several people: he too admires the poet Seamus Heaney and is overjoyed when the poet wins the Nobel Prize. He also likes the work of the writer May Sarton, and when he's at the health club (for which he really had no use), he listens to a Matthew Fox tape. I have always enjoyed reading all three.

We also agree on the painter Edward Hopper. I could never take to Hopper. I find his work depressing in its loneliness and isolation. Nouwen describes his yellow light as cold, whereas Van Gogh's light is spiritual. He read a biography of Hopper only to discover that Hopper was abusive toward his wife. In short, he was a chilling man, and this comes across loudly and clearly in his work.

In his October notes Nouwen openly admits his woundedness:

> The feeling of being abandoned is always around the corner. I keep being surprised at how quickly it rears its ugly head. Yesterday I experienced that nasty feeling in my innermost being. Just raw anxiety, seemingly

disconnected from anything. I kept asking myself, "Why are you so restless, why are you so anxious, why are you so ill at ease, why do you feel so lonely and abandoned?"[21]

It's touching to read that to ease his pain he calls his friend Nathan Ball. Later, he writes, "Soon he called back....Talking lessened my anxiety and I felt peaceful again. No one can ever heal this wound, but when I can talk about it with a good friend I feel better."[22]

Would I ever have the courage to so frankly write about my wounds in a journal I knew someday would be published?

Henri aspired to write narratives. I wonder if he had lived would he have attempted a novel? Perhaps he became weary of the didactic writing he had so beautifully mastered.

Henri's comments on art sent me back to his *Behold the Beauty of the Lord: Praying with Icons*. This is one of my favorite books. It's a simple but beautiful introduction to the spiritual world of icons.

Henri was introduced to the beauty of art at an early age. His mother and father had purchased a small painting by Marc Chagall depicting a simple vase with flowers standing in front of a window. They purchased it long before Chagall was famous. Nouwen grew up with the painting, to the point that he saw it with his "heart's eye," and it offered him much consolation and comfort.

When Henri was in Paris, he and a friend went to the Louvre to view Rembrandt's *The Pilgrims of Emmaus*. If anyone wishes to learn how to *see* art, they should read Henri's description of his museum experience:

> At first sight, the painting was a disappointment. It was much smaller than I had expected and surrounded by so many other paintings that it was hard to see it as a separate work of art. Maybe I was too familiar with it through reproductions to be genuinely surprised.
>
> Jesus sits behind the table looking up in prayer while holding a loaf of bread in his hands. On his right, one of the pilgrims leans backwards with his hands folded; while on his left, the other has moved his chair away from the table and gazes with utter attention at Jesus. Behind him a humble servant, obviously unaware of what is happening, reaches forward to put a plate of food on the table. On the table, a bright white cloth only partially covers the heavy table rug. There are very few objects on the table: three pewter plates, a knife, and two small cups. Jesus sits in front of a majestic stone apse flanked by two big, square pillars. On the right side of the painting, the entrance door is visible, and there is a coat stand in the corner over which a cape has been casually thrown.
>
> The whole painting is in endless varieties of brown: light brown, dark brown, yellow-brown, red-brown, and so on. The source of light is not revealed, but the white tablecloth is the brightest part of the painting.[23]

I would venture to say that the above is the result of acute seeing transformed into prayerful attention. Notice the way the pilgrim looks at Jesus's face "with utter attention." In like manner, Nouwen looked at this painting. He lost himself in the painting. He and his friend, Brad, understood that the painter's purpose was a spiritual one. Brad said, "Now I see that Rembrandt painted the Eucharist, a sacramental event to which we, as we view it, are invited."

That is how I often feel when I read Father Nouwen: in his books, he invites us to a sacramental event. And his invitation goes out to everyone.

I am reminded that Nouwen got into hot water in some Catholic churches (and abbeys) because when he celebrated Mass, he expected everyone to partake of the Holy Eucharist. No one was excluded regardless of what religion he or she was. I don't criticize him for this; in fact, I praise him for it. But I know there are many who wouldn't agree with me.

He understood the restorative power of great works of art. A pious person his whole life, he'd naturally be attracted to holy icons; *Behold the Beauty of the Lord* addresses his favorite four Russian icons, which, he says, he "memorized" as he memorized the Our Father and the Hail Mary in his youth. Their images are deeply imprinted upon his soul and go everywhere with him.

Icons teach us how to be attentive. It is only after long, attentive looking that an icon speaks to the gazer. One must be patient, but the rewards are infinite.

Nouwen says that when prayer becomes difficult, if not impossible, then one should just stand before an icon and gaze. Icons bring us closer to God.

Nouwen's and James Forest's books on icons are valuable lessons on prayer. Every day I stand before my own icon of Christ to pray. My attentive gazing becomes my prayer.

Nouwen writes:

> Icons are not just pious pictures to decorate churches and houses. They are images of Christ and the saints which bring us into contact with the sacred, windows that give us a glimpse of the transcendent. They need to be approached in veneration and with prayer. Only then will they reveal to us the mystery they represent.[24]

And shouldn't this be the way we approach one another? Can't each of us be a window, offering a glimpse of the Christ within us?

Today is another lovely summer day. Temperatures will remain in the 70s and the air is delicious. My lawn is a lush green.

It's painful to read about Henri's nervous breakdown. He luckily had friends to help him move through his terrible darkness. But the image that haunts me is Henri weeping and in a fetal position. His therapists would put him in a bed located in an office and just hug him until he quieted down.

The interruption of his friendship with Nathan Ball caused his breakdown. The importance of this friendship is recorded in his *Spiritual Journals*:

> Over the past few months we have gradually come to know each other. I was not aware of how significant our

relationship had become for me until he left for a month to visit his family and friends in Canada. I missed his presence greatly and looked forward to his return.

Two days ago he came back, and tonight we went out for supper together. I told him that his absence had made me aware of a real affection for him that had grown in me since we had come to know each other. He responded with a strong affirmation of our friendship from his side. As we talked more about past experiences and future plans, it became clear that God had brought us close for a reason.[25]

No matter how you read this selection, it is obvious to me that it is a declaration of love. Surely Ball understood this, and he seemingly handled it quite beautifully.

Art and inspiration. When Henri went to England, he brought along a painting of St. George slaying a dragon. He had psychic dragons to slay and the portrait inspired courage. Well, slaying dragons is not too far-fetched a metaphor for our psychic battles, and Plato says we become what we behold.

I also have been inspired by certain paintings. Salvatore Dali's depiction of Christ at his last meal is one that has moved me many times. Every time I go to Washington D.C., I make my way to the National Gallery to behold it one more time. A copy of that work hung on the walls of my first apartment when I was in my twenties. I've also traveled to New York several times to visit the Frick Museum, the home of Bellini's *St. Francis in Ecstasy*.

Rouault's portraits of Christ have also meant a great deal to me; surely he is one of the greatest painters of the modern era.

Vincent Van Gogh's *Sunflowers* serves as a cover for Nouwen's *Sabbatical Journey*, and Rouault's *Ecce Homo* serves as the cover of *The Wounded Healer*.

Nouwen was ahead of his time in advocating art as a way into a deeper spiritual life. Now we have Sister Wendy saying the same thing. I do like her shows and her insightful commentaries on famous and not so famous art. All that Nouwen and Sister Wendy say is confirmed by Simone Weil who says:"The love of beauty proceeds from God dwelling in our souls and goes out to God present in the universe."[26]

I'm dipping into several of Nouwen's books right now. The one I'm hesitant to read is *The Inner Voice of Love: A Journey Through Anguish to Freedom.* This is the secret journal of his breakdown, and I'm not certain I want or need to read it now. Perhaps I'm afraid of being reminded of my own similar experience, my own dark night of depression when I was totally lost. But I know that before I complete this journal I must face this book and face my memories. Yes, it will be painful, but I agree with Nouwen when he says that we must embrace our wounds for only then do they become gateways to a closer relationship with Christ.

Henri's description of Adam Arnett's (the young disabled man he was assigned to care for at Daybreak) death is immensely moving. My eyes welled with tears. This is the disabled young man who became Henri's beloved, the man who taught him more about the spiritual life than any other person. Upon seeing the deceased Adam, he writes:

> I couldn't keep my eyes from him. I thought, here is the man who more than anyone has connected me with God and the Daybreak community. Here is the man whom I cared for during my first year at Daybreak and have come to love so much. Here is the one I have written about, talked about all over Canada and the United States. Here is my counselor, teacher, and guide, who never could say a word to me but taught me more than anyone else. Here is Adam, my friend, my beloved friend, the most vulnerable of all the people I have ever known and at the same time the most powerful.[27]

Nouwen is here at his most powerful both as a writer and as a loving man, rendered powerful through the humble "weakness" of his beloved Adam.

Nouwen's diaries are ego books: he stands before us warts and all. He seems to be saying, "Take a good look at me as I too am trying to do." He needs to understand himself, to penetrate to his essence.

Like Socrates, I believe the unexamined life isn't worth living. But how much self-scrutiny is enough? I ask this question because there is always the danger of narcissism.

Nouwen received great pleasure from music. He writes movingly about hearing Mahler and the opera *Carmen*. He also played the piano. He loved art, music, and was a great reader. If he hadn't loved Christ so much, pursuing a deeply spiritual life, he could easily have become a worldly aesthete.

If Merton hadn't become a Trappist, I suspect he would've succumbed to a life of jazz clubs, drinking, and writing novels. That is if he could've gotten his first novel published.

Jurjen Beumer's *Henri Nouwen, A Restless Seeking for God* is a good biography—not a great one, because the author doesn't go deeply enough in his efforts to understand Nouwen's restlessness. The definitive biography hasn't been written yet. It's likely that someone will come along, as did Michael Mott with Merton, who will have the disinterestedness necessary to write a top-notch biography. It won't be written, I'm sure, by people who knew Nouwen because he is still perched too high on the pedestal of hero worship.

Beumer says that Nouwen's book *The Return of the Prodigal Son* is Nouwen's most mature work. [28] I agree because by the time Nouwen wrote it he understood more deeply his relationship with his father.

The heat has returned and the humidity. My lawn is beginning to show signs of burnout. No doubt about it, this summer has become hotter, and there's been little rain.

I have written the brochure for my retreat; the front reads:

St. Stephen Priory, Dover, MA
Thomas Merton and Henri Nouwen Retreat
Two Spiritual Guides for Our Time
Day Retreat Directed by Robert Waldron
"Woundedness and the Contemplative Life"

Both Merton and Nouwen are wounded men. Some wounds were inflicted on them when they were infants. They sought cures for their wounds in religious life. Complete cures were never found. As well as they could, they attempted to integrate their wounds; consequently, they were able to establish degrees of wholeness in their lives. Merton overcame his "refusal of women." Nouwen allowed his own parental nature to blossom, to allow himself to touch another human being, through caring for our most needy.

A baffling insight: When I read Nouwen I see more of myself in him than in Merton. Perhaps because I see my own need for constant affirmation. As a teacher I've learned to live without professional affirmation. It simply isn't offered much. Students may write a letter ten years later thanking you for your inspiration or guidance. But that's rare.

The lawyer has tangible affirmation when he wins a case; so does the doctor in a correct diagnosis or successful surgery, the engineer who sees the home or bridge he designed and built. So does the psychologist who sees a patient finally depart, able to face and live his life again. All of this must give professional satisfaction. Teachers, however, must live by hope and faith that what they've taught in their classes will take root and someday flourish. This is especially true of teachers of literature, as I am.

Nouwen wrote *Clowning in Rome*. Like Rouault who painted many clowns during his career, Nouwen is attracted to their humility and their tragedy and the fact that they can make us laugh amid life's absurdity: We must laugh or go mad. Fools for Christ come to mind. What was the name of that awful musical that portrayed Christ as a clown? It came out, I think, about the same time as *Jesus Christ Superstar*, a musical I liked although I didn't agree with its theology (although Andrew Lloyd Webber employed Fulton Sheen's *Life of Christ* as his source).

The title came to me: *Godspell*.

Ninety degree heat again. I made a quick trip to St. Stephen Priory to finalize the retreat date and the cost. Pam, the secretary, suggested forty dollars for the day, which includes breakfast and lunch. I'd like the retreatants to have a full day at the center, starting off with Mass.

Nouwen writes, "Why am I so tired? Although I have all the time I want to sleep, I wake up with an immense feeling of fatigue and get up only because I want to do some work...but everything requires immense effort, and after a few hours of work I collapse in utter exhaustion, often falling into a deep sleep."[29]
Is this his mind or body speaking, or both?

37

A stunning confession in his diary for October 18, "I do not believe that we have to repress our erotic energies in order to live ordered lives. Nor do I believe that we have to give up order and discipline in order to get in touch with the wild energies of existence. But it certainly requires concentrated effort to find our own unique ways to become whole people. The literature and art of the West show that few have accomplished this wholeness. *I certainly have not.*" (emphasis added)[30]

Nouwen may not have achieved wholeness, but he spent a lifetime seeking it. Perhaps the seeking itself is a kind of wholeness for its journey lies in humility. Nouwen seems to say, "I'm fragmented but I seek to be whole, to be whole because I seek peace of mind." Perhaps the secret to wholeness is simply to accept one's self as one is in the *now* moment—not to desire to change anything, only self-acceptance. Perhaps that's the point from which we all have to start: self-acceptance.

Just received from Pam my contract with St. Stephen Priory. They require a minimum number of twenty people as well as a $266 nonrefundable down payment. Again, I'm anxious about having to attract so many people to my retreat. So far I have one commitment. But it's still August. I'll place an ad in the Catholic diocesan paper *The Pilot* in early September when people are likely to have returned from their vacations.

Today is unbearably hot and humid (100 degrees). Not just New England but the whole country is plagued by a heat wave. Last night I kept the air conditioner on all night. My electric bill for this month will be steep.

Nouwen is so down-to-earth. On one page he writes about the beauty of Mozart and on the next he praises the Beatles. He reminds me of Merton who was simultaneously attracted to the highbrow verse of a Rilke or Lorca but also to the lyrics of Bob Dylan and Joan Baez (she once visited him in Gethsemani).

Even into his 60s, Nouwen asks himself, "Why are you so restless, why are you so anxious, why are you so ill at ease, why do you feel so lonely and abandoned?"[31]

It makes me pause again to think about the lack of nurturing he received as an infant. If those years are so pivotal, and I believe they are, how can one ever fill what had not been offered? Thus, I wonder if we are predestined to live out our fate and that no matter what we do, no matter how many right choices we make, no matter how much we will the contrary, we'll never fill what was left empty. A sobering thought.

It comes down to the Christian way of the cross. Christ suffers Calvary. So we too must carry our cross. Something in me, however, says that this is too pat an answer.

Henri identifies with the image of the wounded healer because he knows his wounds. He knows his wounds because he has focused his attention upon them. In fact, he says that in order to help anyone in pain one must first be aware of one's own pain. Awareness leads to hospitality—"hospitality is the ability to pay attention to the guest."[32]

Many times I've remarked that attention is the secret of the inner life. To give attention to another is miraculous because it is selfless. When you gaze upon another with total attention, you (your ego) disappear, for in that moment you are saying to the other: "At this instant in time, you are the most important person in my life, more important than my own self." This is an extraordinary act. It is an act based on choice. The I, before it disappears, must make the decision to step aside for the other.

In our culture such an act is rare and certainly not promulgated. I think of my own students and how assertive and driven they are to succeed at all costs. They compete with each other for everything and winning is the only goal they accept even if it means hurting or stepping on or over a friend. That's what we teach them in our schools: win at all costs. It's practiced in sports and in academics. Humility is a virtue you never hear mentioned. When I do speak of it, I hear snickering from my students. When I ask them what they want from life, they say power, money, and prestige.

As a practicing Christian, Henri Nouwen chose the Other over the I. He understood the cure to his own narcissism. To live at Daybreak and to care for Adam Arnett was the opportunity for his ego to disappear in caring for a totally helpless human being.

Is it a fair assessment to say that Merton desired to disappear into God and Nouwen desired to disappear into another person?

Nouwen's definition of contemplative prayer is "careful attentiveness to One who makes a home in the privileged center of our being gradually leads to recognition."[33] Recognition of what? Of God within ourselves.

Merton was a book-centered contemplative. Nouwen was a people-centered contemplative. When I see the two priests in my mind's eye, I see Merton celebrating Mass alone in his hermitage. I see Nouwen celebrating Mass at a table close to the floor (one he commissioned) surrounded by a number of people.

Jean Vanier offers a beautiful description of the importance of the Eucharist in Nouwen's life:

> Henri found his fullness in the Eucharist. He loved to celebrate the Eucharist and to include everybody in it, and if he sometimes seemed a bit casual with the rules of the Roman Catholic Church concerning intercommunion, it was because he wanted each one present to have a personal encounter with Jesus. Henri loved the Eucharist because he loved Jesus. And he believed passionately in the real presence of Jesus in the consecrated bread and wine. Because the Eucharist was of such a great significance to him, he had a natural talent for making it meaningful, for showing its connectedness to our lives. He would circle the altar, walk out amongst the participants waving his hands here and there. Some people might have found these actions disturbing but they were all expressions of Henri's intense desire to bring people together, around Jesus.[34]

For Merton the exterior holy space was very important. That's why a hermitage was so vital to him. Nouwen was not as attracted to that exterior space; he was focused on the holy space within. In his letters to his nephew Marc, he advises him to "make available the inner space where God can touch you with an all-transforming love."[35]

I'm drawn to his concept of the hospitable heart: We create a hospitable heart by first opening our hearts to everyone who crosses our path. And the key to opening our hearts to others is attention.

Was Henri hospitable to himself? Did he accept into his inner space his homosexual self? Or was this aspect of himself locked in a closet, not allowed into the inner sanctum?

Henri possessed a childlike wonder for the circus, especially for clowns. He's not the only artist who feels this way. I think of Georges Rouault (1871–1958), one of my favorite artists. Henri loved Rouault and several of his books use Rouault's paintings as covers. Rouault had great empathy for clowns. In a letter dated 1905, Rouault describes his personal encounter with the circus world:

> The wagon of nomads halted in the middle of the road, the tottery old horse grazing the sparse grass, the old clown in a corner of his wagon mending his shiny and no longer motley costume; the sharp contrast between shiny, glistening things that are meant to amuse and this exceedingly sad life, at least when observed from afar….Later on, I clearly realized that the clown was myself, he was all of us, almost all of us.[36]

With his artist's eye, Rouault penetrated the clown's mask to see the suffering beneath.

Henri was a master of the happy face. But beneath it lay so much pain.

Henri's description of the circus is similar to Rouault's. He writes:

> The clowns are not the center of events. They appear between great acts, fumble and fall and make us smile again after the tensions created by the heroes we came to admire. The clowns don't have it together…they are awkward, out of balance and left-handed, but…they are on our side. The clowns remind us with a tear and a smile that we are sharing the same human weakness.[37]

I find this description so poignant because Henri himself was so "awkward, out of balance and left-handed."

Merton's best friend, the poet Robert Lax, was also attracted to circus people. I have in front of me now Brother Patrick Hart's *Patmos Journal* with two photographs of Lax; he has a face that reminds me of El Greco: a face long, lean, and bearded—the face of an ascetic.

Lax's reputation as a poet is greater in Europe than it is in the United States. But I have to admit I like his minimalist verse, perhaps because I'm a minimalist myself. Lax's verse eerily captures the circus ambience:

> Have you seen my circus?
> Have you known such a thing?

Did you get up in the early morning and see the wagons
   pull into town?
Did you see them occupy the field?
Were you there when it was set up?
Did you see the cook-house set up in the dark by
   lantern-light?
Did you see them build the fire and sit around it smok-
   ing and talking quietly?[38]

To Lax, circus people are golden people because they offer us
the gift of wonder. Under the big top we are reborn:

(Knowing the wonder to be born of her, hoping to bring
forth a son, a tree, in whose laughing and delicate shade
the children of innocence could rejoice, the field waited.)

A circus is a song of praise,
A song of praise unto the Lord.[39]

With his attention fixed upon the circus, the observer's mind
becomes temporarily vacant of ego, a self-emptying. The emptiness is filled by the presence of something other than ourselves.
Then what happens? Empathy occurs and this leads to nonjudg-
mental compassion. We love clowns because we don't judge them
as foolish: we see ourselves in them and perhaps that's why we
laugh compassionately.

To accept unconditionally another human being in his pain, in
his confusion, in his anger, requires us to be Christlike. And again

it is a matter of choice: we can follow Christ or not follow him. We can choose to live the parable of the Prodigal Son or not to live it.

Gazing upon art is one way to teach people how to be attentive. When Nouwen traveled to Russia to gaze upon Rembrandt's *The Return of the Prodigal Son*, he went not merely as a museum patron. His purpose was, of course, aesthetic but also deeply spiritual. Or perhaps it's better to say that at first his experience was aesthetic, for indeed it was the beauty of the painting that first attracted him. Then the painting's message intrigued him to the point that he lost himself in gazing upon it. The gazing led to the articulation of what he contemplated.

For my retreat I'd like a huge poster-board copy of this painting. I'll use it as a focus to illustrate Nouwen's spiritual way. Perhaps I'll open a discussion based upon this one painting and upon Nouwen's book.

Today I read that Hillary Clinton has read Nouwen's *Prodigal Son* and is recommending it to everyone, especially to people going through a difficult time.

Amazing!

I have to laugh at Henri at the supermarket. After paying his bill, he applies for an "advantage" card and returns to lead his cart to his car. However, when he arrives at the door, he notices articles he doesn't remember purchasing. He'd absentmindedly had taken someone else's cart![40]

I can't picture Merton at a supermarket.

Nouwen thinks a lot about death. He wonders how long he'll live. He decides, "Every day should be well lived."[41]

Henri was most happy when he celebrated Mass with friends. His description of Mass at his friend Robert Jonas's Empty Bell, a Zen meditation room, is one filled with joy.

The Nouwen books I'll focus on for my retreat are *Genesee Diary, Sabbatical Journey, The Return of the Prodigal Son, Behold the Beauty of the Lord, Praying with Icons,* and his "secret" journal, *The Inner Voice of Love.* This is more than enough for the morning session. I think I'll open the day with a general statement about Merton and Nouwen and their affinities.

Today I had a poster-board made of Rembrandt's *The Return of the Prodigal Son.* It will be useful when I address Nouwen's thoughts about praying with icons.

Icons also helped Nouwen face his depression; they offered him the opportunity to lose himself in a holy space where he was refreshed and consoled. He began his love affair with icons in Trosly-Breuil, France, when someone had placed an icon of the Holy Trinity on his desk. He found himself repeatedly drawn to focus his attention on the icon; his attention became prayer and his prayer eventually was articulated in his lovely book *Behold the Beauty of the Lord.*

Henri's identification with the wounded healer resonates with me. Why is it that so many people expect their priests to be perfect? It's ironic that our two greatest spiritual writers were so obviously wounded men. Merton and Nouwen were lonely men who had great difficulty connecting *intimately* with other people. Merton was never able to connect with a woman, later confessing to his "refusal of women." Nouwen, attracted to men, was never able to come to terms with his homosexuality.

I am moved by the story of Nouwen's attending with a friend the movie *Maurice* based on E. M. Forster's novel of the same name. Forster's novel was published posthumously because he feared knowledge of his homosexuality would likely have hurt his career. After the movie, Nouwen broke down and wept uncontrollably.

I must read the book and see the movie to understand why Nouwen reacted so emotionally. I suspect he saw himself in one of the characters.

Is homosexuality a wound? Or is it the result of a wound?

Shame on me to use such a pejorative term ("wound") for homosexuality! I am my conditioning.

Henri's physical awkwardness is revelatory. When he was hit by a truck, he was injured severely (lost his spleen). He didn't feel, I suspect, at home with/in his body, thus his resultant physical ineptitude. His body was wounded in his infancy when his mother refused to nurture and to caress it. Perhaps he grew up feeling that this "thing," the body, was somehow shameful. Consequently, he focused his life thereafter on the soul, the spiritual. The typical Platonic split: body bad, spirit good. The untold harm by such a too often accepted and unquestioned duality!

His fascination with the trapeze artists, the Rodleighs, makes sense. He not only admired their artistry, but on some level he must have been fascinated by their total acceptance of the power and beauty of their bodies. They were physically what he was spiritually: grace-full.

Today I went to Barnes and Noble to purchase Eugene Kennedy's *The Unhealed Wound*. While looking for it, I came across a newly published book: *Befriending Life: Encounters with Henri Nouwen*. One copy was left on the shelf, and I grabbed it. Just a few moments ago I finished Nathan Ball's essay on his friendship with Nouwen, "A Covenant of Friendship." What a tribute to Nouwen! Ball is frank about the friendship and its stormy ups and downs. But what comes through to this reader is Ball's love for Nouwen. Ball is careful to mention that he is heterosexual; he states that he was "safe" for Nouwen to love. His exact comment, "As a heterosexual man I was a safe person for Henri to love deeply, and I in turn was eager for his friendship and companionship."[42]

Surely Ball's sexual orientation had little to do with Nouwen's love for him. One can't predict who one will fall in love with. I daresay no one chooses by a consideration of the other's sexuality. Predetermination of this sort doesn't fit in with my definition of love. Nouwen likely loved Ball for the totality of his person, of which his sexual persuasion was only a fragment of the whole.

I've placed my ad for my retreat in the Catholic paper. Visiting the priory, I found that most of my brochures had been taken so I replenished the supply. So far I have two commitments, one from

48

a former Trappist who studied under Merton. He's now married and lives on Cape Cod. The other is Dorothy, my friend from the Merton Chapter. She attends all my lectures and is a faithful friend I am so lucky to have.

Just read Rodleigh Stevens's essay "Henri with the Circus," a beautiful tribute to Henri who found a temporary home with them.

Yes, community life drew Henri, but no matter what community he joined, whether it was the Trappists, Daybreak, the circus, he would have to be the star. To simply disappear was not an option for him. Or rather it was an option, but one he rejected.

I've had time to think about Rodleigh's essay about Henri. Rodleigh Stevens was the leader of the trapeze act called the Flying Rodleighs; the group also included his wife, sister, and several other people. Henri met them in 1991 and fell in love with their act.

Henri kept a lot of notes and tapes of interviews because he intended to write a book about the trapeze act. He never wrote the book although he did narrate an English-language version of *Angels over the Net*, a documentary about the troupe.

Henri was fascinated by the total trust between the flier and the catcher. There is that ever-so-brief time when the flier is suspended in the air alone, just about to be caught by the catcher. It is a moment of total surrender and trust.

Henri likely saw God as our divine catcher, and we, if willing, the fliers. How many of us have the courage to be fliers?

I borrowed the film *Maurice* from the library. It is a well-acted and poetically crafted film with homosexual love as its theme. Two men, Maurice and Clive, fall in love. Maurice loves completely, but Clive is ashamed and rejects his nature. In the end, Clive abandons Maurice for marriage.

I am reminded of T. S. Eliot's line said by Thomas Becket, "to do the right deed for the wrong reason."[43] When Merton heard that line he broke down in tears, and Henri wept after seeing *Maurice*. Two intriguing emotional outbursts.

In imitation of Nouwen, I'm living with Rembrandt's painting. It is before me this moment. I hope I can somehow vicariously experience what Nouwen did when he gazed upon it for so many hours and so many days. Who is the barely visible woman in the upper left hand corner? I must check to see if Nouwen hazards a guess.

I made another visit to the priory with my cousin, Donna, who is from the West Coast. I told her to walk around while I went in search of the secretary, Pam, who wasn't in her office. When I returned, I found Donna quietly sitting in the main parlor. She seemed quite happy soaking in the silence. She described the chapel as "non-Catholic."

"How?" I asked.

"Without stained-glass windows, it reminds me of Protestant churches."

Of course, she's right. But the ever-burning vigil light before the tabernacle is all that's needed to identify a Catholic church.

On the other hand, Donna is literary and instantly understood what I had meant by Manderley, when I described St. Stephen's tree-arched entrance. She'd read Daphne du Maurier's book *Rebecca* many years ago—and saw Alfred Hitchcock's movie version.

In Eugene Kennedy's new, ground-breaking book *The Unhealed Wound*, he devotes a chapter to Thomas Merton and his affair with his nurse. He is somewhat harsh in his judgment: Merton was too willing to dump her if he had to, and he seemingly burned her letters without a trace of remorse.

Henri, as far as I know from what I've read, didn't experience this kind of erotic love. When a woman friend asked Henri whether or not he was having an erotic relationship with the male friend he'd talked about, Henri bristled and reminded her that he was a celibate.[44]

School starts next week. And the retreat is closer. I don't feel that I have a handle on Nouwen. I must devote myself to a marathon reading—re-read all the books I've chosen and perhaps re-read the two biographies—all in search of new insights. And it is now time to read his secret journal. I've put this off too long.

School begins on Wednesday, and I'm still readying myself for my October retreat. This week I've accomplished much reading, including Peggy Rosenthal's (of *The Poets' Jesus* fame) manuscript *Praying the Gospels through Poetry*. Writing a blurb for her book was a pleasure. Her book is inspiring, and I hope it does well.

Well, I finally have begun Nouwen's *The Inner Voice of Love*. The first entry describes his woundedness: "There is a deep hole in your being, like an abyss."[45] Nouwen forces himself to face this abyss by not averting his eyes. The Medusa turns men into stone if they gaze directly upon her; only oblique gazing protects the viewer. For gazing into the abyss, a direct look is necessary; otherwise, how will we ever become *hospitable*, as Nouwen repeatedly advises, to our inner wounds? I say hospitable because many wounds won't go away; they are part of the permanent furniture of our inner being.

Nouwen suggests that all his life he was a "pleaser." He needed to please everyone and exhausted himself in the process. Knowing this about himself and the fact that he will likely continue to be a pleaser may lead to more self-acceptance. And if he knows why he's always been a pleaser, then perhaps he may be able to cease being a victim to it.

Nouwen sees his divided self: part of him is filled by God; another part needs human affirmation and love.

In his deepest heart's core, Nouwen knows God loves him. The doubt he suffers from is focused on the fact that Nouwen doesn't really think he's lovable. Merton had the same problem, and it didn't disappear until his affair with his nurse. Nouwen had no erotic love affair as far as I know. But I wonder if it would have liberated him.

Carl Jung would describe Nouwen as a man who never lived out his instinctual life.

Perhaps the greatest thing that Nouwen learned during his breakdown is that no person can meet all our needs. Some needs are satisfied only by God.

Man was not meant to be alone. So much truth to that. Even Christ was surrounded by men and women. Yet in the end he was abandoned and suffered alone.

When Nouwen felt alone and abandoned, he turned to Christ. Who better to turn to?

I came to a stop when I read the following from *Inner Voice*, "Home is where you are truly safe. It is where you can receive what you desire. You need human hands to hold you there so you don't run away again."[46]

I am impressed by two things: Nouwen's constant theme of finding a home and his many references to hands throughout his work. He himself is said to have had very large and expressive hands. That's what I remember most from seeing him speak in Cambridge when he used his hands to get across his message, and did so eloquently.

I am now looking at Rembrandt's *Return of the Prodigal Son*; the father's hands lovingly rest upon the son's back, recently so burdened with life's vicissitudes. These are radiant hands through which pour the father's love for his once dead son who again lives.

Such are the hands that Father Nouwen craved to be touched by, perhaps by his own father. Nouwen's writings suggest that his father wasn't affectionate. But when Nouwen was hospitalized after being hit by a car, his father came all the way from Holland to be with him. Many things were said that had to be said by father and son. I hope it was enough to satisfy this "prodigal" son.

Our relationship with our parents: therein lies our joys and likely our despairs.

I've been reading Matthew's Gospel. Because of my daily contact with Henri, references to seeing and touching leaped up at me:

> "Look at the birds of the sky—they neither sow nor gather into barns…Look how the lilies of the field grow; they neither work nor spin." (Matt 6:26–30)

> Jesus reached out his hand, touched him [a leper], and said, "I do wish it, be made clean!" (Matt 8:3–4)

> He touched her [Peter's mother] and the fever left her. (Matt 8:14–15)

> Jesus touched their [the blind men] eyes and said, "Let it be done to you according to your faith!" and their eyes were opened. (Matt 9:29–31)

> Jesus said, "Although they look, they don't see. But blessed are your eyes because they see, and your ears because they hear." (Matt 13:13-14, 16)[47]

I am pleased that I recently purchased the St. Paul Catholic Edition of the Bible—a handsome edition. Although I love my King James and New Jerusalem Bibles, I prefer St. Paul's large print. Surely another sign of my aging!

I am moved by the leper who says, "Lord, if you wish to, you can make me clean." Jesus says, "I wish to." I like this translation more than "I am willing." To wish shows the real love Jesus has for the ill man. And Jesus wishes to touch us all, to heal us all. Even without our asking.

If we truly believe that God loves us unconditionally, that he is closer to us than we are to ourselves, that he loves us more than we could ever love ourselves, then how could we ever succumb to despair?

Do we really believe it?

Is it fair or even right to ask a man who elects to become a priest to live the rest of his life touch-deprived? I'm not only talking about the erotically charged touch; I mean the simple touch of hand to hand, the caress across the cheek, the touch that tousles the hair, the touch that comforts and soothes.

Priests live without touch. Surely Nouwen would have been a happier man if he'd been the recipient of more touch in his life. Human touch, such a simple thing and taken for granted by most, but for vowed celibates it is sacrificed to God. Would God ask for such a deprivation? I think of Christ and his willingness to touch all: sinners, the ill, the blind, little children—what is most human about the stories of Christ is that he touched—with his hand, with his eyes, with his attention, with his compassion, with his love.

School started today and I have a full schedule. In fact, I have roughly the same number of students I had when I started to teach thirty-three years ago. But we have a new cafeteria and a newly built library. The books, I'm told, will come. But not to worry, we have computers!

I'm getting very anxious about attracting enough people for my retreat. I tell myself not to worry, but I'm not sleeping as well as I usually do.

Having written three books about Merton, it's a bit ironic that I feel less secure about what I want to say about Merton's woundedness than I do about Nouwen's. And it's obvious why: Nouwen wrote much about his wounds, Merton little. Yet it was through Merton that Nouwen was briefly attracted to monastic life because like Merton he needed a laboratory for his experiment in living.

We experiment in life in order to find the right environment to help us to find our True Self. Merton failed within the walls of Cambridge University but succeeded at Columbia. But Columbia proved only to be his apprenticeship. Within the walls of Gethsemani in Kentucky, he found the right *container* to continue his experiment of finding the True Self. He probably unconsciously knew he needed an authoritarian structure to keep him from his own self-destructive tendencies.

Nouwen looked for a *container* that would fit his refined temperament. He had a more difficult time finding it than Merton. Nouwen's years spent in academia were not wasted, but such a cerebral world was not what he needed. He needed a place where he could touch and be touched—a world that was safe, not sexually alluring. He found it in Daybreak. The crack in the container occurred when Nouwen fell in love with another Daybreak volunteer/worker. This was unexpected. But like Merton with his falling in love with his nurse, Nouwen's falling in love may have been the best thing to have happened to him.

Henri's most agonizing wound: his feeling of emptiness when he realizes "the absence of the love you most desire."[48] He could be referring to Nathan Ball or God.

The Inner Voice of Love is painful to read because I don't quite believe Nouwen when he says God's love is first; therefore, it's above all human love. I suspect he's trying to convince himself about this. Nouwen's need for people's love, however, is so very human, so very understandable, so very necessary.

First a priest, then a man? Or is it first a man, then a priest?

Nouwen's secret journal entries are as anguished as Gerard Manley Hopkins's terrible sonnets. Both were homosexual priests who battled their natures. Both suffered from depression. When Nouwen admits he cannot cure himself, he's being honest. He can't *cure* his sexual nature.

It's a soul-rending confrontation: his homosexual nature versus his conditioned Catholic self. A war of body versus soul. And seemingly Nouwen's spirit won. The power of grace!

But the cost!

This week PBS repeated its 1982 production of Evelyn Waugh's *Brideshead Revisited*. Sebastian Flyte is a character filled with self-hatred—he hates what he is: a homosexual. His only escape is alcohol and thus he becomes a dissipated drunk.

The root of the conflict, of course, was his Catholicism and his sexual nature. His remark to Charles Ryder says it all, "I am ashamed of myself."

I'm reading Etty Hillesum's *An Interrupted Life*, her diaries written in Holland between 1941 and 1943. They are riveting in their erotic candidness. She too is battling her highly erotic nature and more often than not she succumbs to it. Yet she is a highly spiritual woman. Like Nouwen, she knows no man can ever fulfill her needs. She writes, "Growing more and more certain that there is no help or assurance or refuge in others."[49] Like Merton and Nouwen, she recognizes the universal craving for a home; she says, "Everyone seeks a home, a refuge."[50] The implication is Augustinian: "Our hearts are restless until they rest in Thee."

I am the moderator of our reading club's discussion of Hillesum's diaries. Most of the members are women. How shall I address her eroticism? She is so frank about her desires, her needs, her hungers. Unlike Nouwen, she is not deprived of touch, of caresses, and of kisses from her lover S. Perhaps I should just let the members read aloud the sections that moved them, and if they happen to be her erotic episodes, well, let it be.

The more I think of Nouwen's touch-impoverished infancy, the more it makes sense that he decided to choose Daybreak. There he took care of Adam: he fed him, bathed him, dressed him, combed his hair, brushed his teeth; in short, he did for him what a loving parent would do for an infant. Nouwen did for Adam what was not done for him; thus, he vicariously does for himself what he craved as a child. This compensation doesn't diminish his love for Adam, but I'm sure Nouwen would be the first to admit that his own needs were vicariously being met— and in a profound way.

I am struck by the fact that Etty Hillesum and Henri Nouwen lived not far from one another in Holland in the early 1940s when she was 27 and Nouwen was about 10. Two diarists: one to become internationally known as a Catholic priest, the other to be world famous as a Jewish intellectual of great promise murdered in a concentration camp, a woman whose diaries would survive to tell her haunting story.

I received an e-mail from Peggy Rosenthal today. She was shocked by the information about Nouwen's rearing. She described how loved and touched her grandchild is. I wrote back that her grandchild is fortunate and blessed. She also commented on how amazing it was that Nouwen turned out as sane as he did. Yes, that is remarkable.

When I think of Nouwen's infancy, I think of Shakespeare's "Sweet are the uses of adversity." We examined this very line in class today. My students had difficulty with the passage until I realized they didn't understand the meaning of *adversity*. I'd taken it for granted that my gifted students would know it! I was recently told that today's kids are impoverished by as many as 10,000 words compared to my generation. If it's true. it's alarming!

But once they understood the meaning of that one word, they instantly flew toward understanding what Shakespeare meant. It all came down to compensation, as one student suggested: we compensate for what we have missed or suffered in life. Smart kid. So Nouwen found what he needed in his ministry, and because he was so wounded, he was able to reach out to others and to help them move through it.

Altruistic compensation.

My ad appeared in the local Catholic paper, but no takers on my retreat. This is really nerve-racking. But I must still continue to prepare myself.

Late summer light after dinner. I just sat and observed the twilight illumine my Linden tree. A deep golden light. The sky was so clearly blue, and there was a warm breeze—makes one glad to be alive. Not ecstasy, but joy in beauty observed.

There are not many nature descriptions in Nouwen's journals. Merton becomes more aware of nature's beauty in his later journals. Etty was seemingly aware of beauty all the time. In fact, her descriptions are more poignant because the reader knows that she will soon die. She is a luminous spirit. All three diarists are luminous but in different ways. But it is Etty who lived out her erotic life; of the three, she is the most well-balanced. Because of her erotic life? I am inclined to say yes.

Today the terrorist acts against the New York World Trade Center and the U.S. Pentagon occurred. A sad day for America. A sad day for the world.

For a week I couldn't do much but stare at the television and pray along with the rest of the country for survivors. But there were so few. Churches, temples, and mosques across the nation are crowded with the faithful turning to God, all trying to understand this evil that has murdered so many innocent men, women, and children.

I've just finished reading Nouwen's book *Reaching Out*. It was written during his time at Yale. It's a useful book that outlines the three movements of the spiritual journey:

The Journey from Loneliness to Solitude
The Journey from Hostility to Hospitality
The Journey from Illusion to Prayer

This is a model that helps me understand Father Nouwen's quest for union with God.

Loneliness is quite different from solitude. It is a state of not being connected to anyone. Nouwen says it is "one of the most universal sources of human suffering today."[51]

I spend much time alone, but I do so from choice. The longer I live the more I desire to be alone for only then do I have the time to spend in prayer. When the phone rings, I occasionally don't want to pick it up: I have less tolerance for chatter and gossip, which, I find, takes up too much of my time. But I need to talk with friends; it's a way of connecting with them and with relatives.

Nouwen's phone was always ringing, and he answered it. Other people's woes took up much of his time. He needed to be needed. But eventually even he needed time to be alone; thus, he twice went off for long stays with the Trappists at Genesee.

Basically, he was a lonely man. He learned that no human being could fill all his needs, yet he still longed for a special friend.

Although Merton became a hermit, I can't envisage Nouwen as one. The very notion makes me smile. Periodically, Nouwen needed to get away, to take stock, to re-energize himself, to write, to think, just to be. In *Reaching Out*, when he writes about solitude, he quotes Thomas Merton, a connoisseur par excellence of silence and solitude.

The paradox of solitude is that separation from each other often leads to a greater communion.

Nouwen says we must respect the solitude of others. We do this by allowing them the space to be themselves without the imposition of our own egotistical demands.

God is the model in this: God gives us the space to be, to choose the kind of person we wish to become. No coercion, only absolute freedom.

But so often Nouwen didn't practice what he preached.

But is it good for man to be alone too much? Merton did too much drinking in the hermitage. Had he perhaps overestimated the value of the solitary life or underestimated himself and his needs for communal life?

The second movement of the spiritual journey (from Hostility to Hospitality) addresses self-rejection and the importance of hospitality. Nouwen says that we must learn to accept ourselves; in fact, we must love ourselves. Only then can we be hospitable to our neighbor. He sees hospitality as a virtue founded on poverty of the heart, which is achieved when the self is forgotten. And the self is forgotten in an act of attention. To give our attention to another is to become empty of our own selfishness, to be empty so that we can receive others into our heart. *A person then becomes a host.*

Nouwen's teaching on hospitality reminds me of George Herbert's poem, "Love Bade Me Welcome," a poem Simone Weil called the most beautiful poem in the world.

> Love bade me welcome: yet my soul drew back,
>   Guiltie of dust and sinne,
> But quick-ey'd Love, observing me grow slack
>   From my first entrance in,
> Drew nearer to me, sweetly questioning,
>   If I lack'd any thing.[52]

Deirdre LaNoue's *The Spiritual Legacy of Henri Nouwen* is a very insightful, critical commentary (and the first I know of) on Nouwen's life and work. Her remarks on Nouwen's commitment to celibacy are arresting: "Although Nouwen never openly admitted a struggle with homosexuality in his writing or speaking, his closest friends knew that he did struggle with it. In the midst of this torturous struggle, however, Nouwen was committed to his vow of celibacy and wanted to be obedient in every way to Christ….His struggle to recover emotional health after a friendship with a man became too emotionally possessing was revealed in *The Inner Voice of Love*, though homosexuality is never mentioned."[53]

For a man who was so acutely transparent about his life, why did he hide his sexual nature? Was it shame? Or self-preservation? I think perhaps it was a combination of both. Would he have become the world renowned spiritual teacher if everyone had known he was a homosexual? Would he have been invited to Notre Dame, Yale, and Harvard? Would he have been invited to Daybreak? Would he have been published by the Catholic press?

I've lived with Henri Nouwen for more than ten weeks now, and I've come to understand that the center of his spiritual life is Christ. His love for Jesus is everywhere evident. Nouwen writes, "Jesus has to be and to become ever more the center of my life. It is not enough that Jesus is my teacher, my guide, my source of inspiration. It is not even enough that he is my companion on the journey, my friend and my brother. Jesus must become the heart of my heart, the fire of my life, the love of my soul, the bridegroom of my spirit. He must become my only thought, my only desire."[54]

Surely with today's World Trade Center towers and Pentagon tragedies, Nouwen would be in the middle offering prayers, hope, and encouragement. His large hands and heart would've reached out to everyone. He would've been a calm voice asking for peace and love. He would warn us not to hate the *enemy*; he would've reminded us all that we are children of God no matter our religion, ethnicity, skin color, or nationality.

Father Nouwen would say:

> I cannot take your pain away, I cannot offer you a solution for your problem, but I can promise you that I won't leave you alone and will hold on to you as long as I can.[55]

Well, the checks are finally coming in for registration. I'm certain of at least ten people for the retreat. The minimum is twenty, but I have several more weeks to reach my quota. I'm getting more and more sure of myself about Nouwen. I know the direction I want to take. My retreat title is "Woundedness and the Contemplative Life." I will address the woundedness of both Nouwen and Merton and how they found the *cure* for their wounds in prayer.

What many people don't know is that both men underwent psychological therapy. Nouwen's was extensive, especially when he had his breakdown over Nathan Ball. Merton also went to a psychiatrist, but nullified its worth by becoming friends with him.

Our wounds are a blessing when they allow others to act as the balm. If anything is proven by our recent tragedy, it is that the death of all those innocent people has brought out the great generosity and love of the American people who want to help the victims in any way they can. One can't help being moved by our nation's response to such deliberate wounding of fellow Americans.

Nouwen understood in a deep way that his own woundedness would help him be more compassionate to all the wounded he met during his life. He was familiar with the space of woundedness and could enter it and not be frightened by it. Ground Zero would not have terrified him. He also knew the needed gestures, the needed words, the needed silence. And yet so often he felt that he himself didn't receive the longed-for gestures and words, often feeling abandoned, neglected, and rejected.

Fulton Sheen said that there are three kinds of love: Eros, Philia, and Agape. Nouwen experienced Philia with his many friends. He believed in Agape, God's unconditional love for each of us and lived his life according to that belief. But I suspect it was Eros, the love that includes the erotic, that he likely craved most. And that was his greatest sacrifice. I also suspect he never realized what the cost would be to him physically, psychologically, and spiritually.

From all that I've read about Nouwen, I find no evidence that he ever lived out his instinctual life. Perhaps he was a virgin his whole life. Merton, on the other hand, lived an Augustinian youth. Two wounded men who turned toward God's love.

I mentioned the three kinds of love to my secondary students the other day while we were analyzing Shakespeare's play *As You Like It*, a play of gender bending par excellence. They were very intrigued by the idea of Philia, love of friends. They had not thought that they loved their friends. One student said in a somewhat defiant way, "I like my friends but I don't love them." I said, "No one should feel ashamed of loving." A hush lingered in the air, suggesting that my students had perhaps recognized a truth they never understood before. But the moment was shattered by the sounding bell, ending the period.

Nouwen critic Deirdre LaNoue says:

> A second aspect that contributed to Nouwen's unique ability to relate to the American culture was his accessibility. Thomas Merton will remain the most influential voice of the twentieth century in the area of Christian spirituality. He was a literary and philosophical genius

as well as a contemplative and social critic. Nouwen's style of communication was more simple and direct. He never used long or complicated arguments and his books were short monographs for the most part. I do not mean to imply that he lacked depth or was rudimentary. On the contrary, Nouwen's messages were challenging and creative. Yet Nouwen's work appealed to a wide variety of readers because they could easily grasp his messages and find their own story in reading his.[56]

I agree with LaNoue's assessment. I'd just add one thing: Nouwen's genius was his own transparency. Merton aimed for transparency and sometimes achieved it. Nouwen didn't have to try: it was very much a part of his personality.

I wish Henri had had the chance to write the two books he planned: one on human sexuality and the other on the flying Rodleighs. The Rodleighs represented physical beauty and grace. He also saw theology in their trapeze act. As I already mentioned, there is a moment when the flier is totally suspended in air with the absolute trust that he will be caught by his partner. It is a paradigm for the kind of trust we should place in God, to trust that he too will catch us.

The leap of faith is often linked with darkness, but it also occurs in the light.

In the *Inner Voice of Love*, Nouwen says that the True Self hears God saying, "You are accepted."[57] I am reminded of Paul Tillich's famous sermon where he says the same thing, "Simply accept the fact that you are accepted!"[58] When I first read Tillich's homily, I wept tears of joy because for so long I had tried to be the perfect Catholic and here was a Protestant reminding me that God accepts me now as I am.

Nouwen's life was a search for acceptance. He believed God accepted him, but I suspect he didn't believe people did. Or at least some people, and for a man who craved affirmation, any rejection was unbearable.

Pam from the priory called. Seems there's another retreat going on the same day as mine, a retreat for nuns. The nuns requested permission to sit in on my Nouwen/Merton retreat and needed to know how much it would cost. I don't have the heart to charge the nuns. I'm pleased that they're interested. The more the merrier.

I am now preparing my retreatants' folders. I've included a life chronology and bibliography for both Nouwen and Merton. I've also included certain selections from their writings. I'm boldly including four of Merton's love poems to M. And I added a few selections from Father Nouwen's *The Inner Voice of Love*, which I think is his most revelatory writing. But as revelatory as it is, it leaves much in shadow.

I've been again closely studying Rembrandt's *The Return of the Prodigal Son*. I'm trying to see it with Father Nouwen's eyes. What did he see? And why did it resonate so much for him that he had to travel to Russia to view the original?

Obviously, he sees himself in the painting. He writes of the father in the painting:

> The dim-eyed old father holds his returned son close to his chest with an unconditional love. Both of his hands, one strong and masculine, the other gentle and feminine, rest on his son's shoulders. He does not look at his son but feels his young, tired body and lets him rest in his embrace. His immense red cape is like the wings of a mother bird covering her fragile nestling. He seems to think only one thing: "He is back home, and I am so glad to have him with me again."
>
> So why delay? God is standing there with open arms, waiting to embrace me. He won't ask any questions about my past. Just having me back is all he desires.[59]

From a Jungian perspective, I think I understand the painting. All the characteristic obscurity (*chiaroscuro*) of the painting represents the unconscious, especially that aspect of the psyche that Jung describes as the shadow. There was so much of Nouwen's shadow not revealed during his lifetime, perhaps because he was afraid to bring it into the light of day (consciousness). His biographer Michael Ford writes at length about Nouwen's friends recommending that he come out of the closet—a recommendation he flatly refused.

And that female figure who hovers above the Prodigal Son and his father, she represents, I believe, the unintegrated anima, those feminine aspects of the personality that must be integrated in order to achieve psychological wholeness.

Nouwen remained too cerebral. By this I mean that he was always in the process of writing a book about his experiences. Perhaps he was too quick to intellectualize his experiences before living through them thoroughly. He didn't allow himself to be free of his writing, grasping too tightly onto the written word. Some will say that his writing was his lifesaver without which he would've drowned. Nevertheless, what would have happened if he had let go of his self-image as a writer—for just a short time?

I've just come across another remarkable example of Nouwen's intense appreciation of art. He truly had the eye of an art aficionado. When he was in Germany, he visited the Augustiner Museum in Freiburg where he encountered one of the most moving Christ figures he'd ever seen, the *Christus auf Palmesel* ("Christ on the Palm-Donkey"). He writes of this sculpture:

> Christ's long, slender face with a high forehead, inward-looking eyes, long hair, and a small forked beard expresses the mystery of his suffering in a way that holds me spellbound. As he rides into Jerusalem surrounded by people shouting "hosanna," cutting branches from the trees and spreading them in his path (Matthew 21:18), Jesus appears completely concentrated on something else. He does not look at the excited crowd. He does not wave. He sees beyond all the noise and movement to what is ahead of him: an agonizing journey of betrayal, torture, crucifixion, and death. His unfocused eyes see what nobody around him can see; his high forehead

reflects a knowledge of things to come far beyond anyone's understanding.

There is melancholy, but also peaceful acceptance. There is insight into the fickleness of the human heart, but also immense compassion. There is a deep awareness of the unspeakable pain to be suffered, but also a strong determination to do God's will. Above all, there is love, an endless, deep, and far-reaching love born of an unbreakable intimacy with God and reaching out to all people wherever they are, were, or will be. There is nothing that he does not fully know. There is nobody whom he does not fully love.[60]

The above is pure meditation. Father Nouwen shows what it's like to lose oneself in beauty. He also brings art alive for the reader, the way Sister Wendy does for so many people. Art is for everyone and not just the critics.

If I learn to appreciate art with half of Nouwen's insight, I'll feel that I've accomplished something rare.

Art and prayer: Several years ago I had the good fortune for fifteen minutes to gaze upon Michelangelo's Pieta at the Bargello in Florence. Miraculously, there were no other tourists to interrupt me, and I felt I was alone with Christ. It was time I'll never forget. And I was so moved because it was Michelangelo himself holding Christ's crucified body, not Mary—Michelangelo's anima allowed to come forth.

I've sometimes imagined myself bearing Christ's body....

I've decided to begin my retreat with a reading of my essay "Broken into Beauty," which addresses the theme of *woundedness*— what it means to be wounded and to be shaped by it.

Meditating on Rembrandt's painting, I'm reminded of one of Jung's most eloquent passages, one about forgiveness. I can't remember in what book I read it. I must find it.

I found it. Jung writes:

> Simple things are always the most difficult. In actual life it requires the greatest art to be simple, and so acceptance of oneself is the essence of the moral problem and the acid test of one's whole outlook on life. That I feed the beggar, that I forgive an insult, that I love my enemy in the name of Christ—all these are undoubtedly great virtues. What I do unto the least of my brethren, that I do unto Christ. But what if I should discover that the least amongst them all, the poorest of all beggars, the most impudent of all offenders, yea the fiend himself— that these are within me, and that I myself stand in need of the alms of my own kindness, that I myself am the enemy who must be loved—what then?[61]

Today is an exquisite October day, quite different from yesterday's blustery weather. The predicted frost didn't occur so my mums and petunias still proclaim their beauty. Of all the months, I prefer October, both its glorious beauty and its sadness. We can't escape the reality of death. Wallace Stevens writes, "Death is the mother of all beauty."[62]

I've finally encountered someone who had met Nouwen. Dr. Edward Gray attended Mass celebrated by Nouwen at Robert Jonas's house in nearby Watertown. Dr. Gray is an eminent surgeon, a member of the medical team responsible for the first organ transplantation at Boston's Peter Bent Brigham Hospital in 1954.

He says the Mass was spiritually uplifting; he writes:

> Mass at Robert Jonas's with Henri Nouwen. Mary Fran and I attended with eight other people. We sat on the floor around a low table. This was the most powerful Mass I've ever experienced. The word "powerful" doesn't begin to describe its beauty. Father Nouwen opens his spirit to the presence of God, and we too are opened to it by his luminous (and yes, numinous) example.
>
> When he held up the host in his large, expressive hands, I felt the reality of the body and blood of Christ present with us through the mystery of transubstantiation. A Mass I shall never forget. Mary Fran [his wife] felt the same.[63]

Dr. Gray offered to introduce me to Nouwen's friend Robert Jonas, but I declined. I said that I didn't want to lose my objectivity or have my opinions colored by someone who knew Nouwen. When I said this, I immediately felt that I sounded ungrateful but when Dr. Gray's wife, Mary Fran, nodded in agreement, I knew she understood me.

I am helping to edit Dr. Gray's spiritual memoir. His colleague and friend Dr. Joseph Murray, who won the Nobel Prize in Medicine in 1990, has just published his autobiography *Surgery of the Soul*. I noticed Dr. Murray's book in the Harvard Coop the other day: an impressive book with an impressive price: $35!

Dr. Gray's book is not straight autobiography but more of a spiritual memoir. He is a kind man whose goodness radiates from his face. His spiritual life is grounded in centering prayer as espoused by Father Thomas Keating, the well-known Trappist writer and retreat master.

I met Father Keating at St. Joseph's Abbey in the early 1970s. I knew immediately I was in the presence of a holy man. I feel the same way about Dr. Gray.

My friend Pauline Grogan has called me from New Zealand. She has decided to leave teaching. She can't tolerate another year of school politics. It's too sad because she is such a gifted and sensitive teacher and the kids will lose out. But I support her in her decision. She has already written one volume of autobiography (well received in New Zealand) and now she will embark on a book about James Lynch, a man who lay in a hospital bed for four decades. She says he was a saint and even though he was paralyzed and couldn't speak, he became her spiritual advisor. James Lynch's story is one everyone should know about and Pauline is the one to write his story.

Teaching has recently become nearly intolerable for me. Today's students are difficult to motivate. Even my best efforts to stimulate them often fail. Either I've lost the magic touch I once had to bring a class to life or I just don't understand today's kids.

They are indeed candid and tell me they don't like to read. They don't want to "waste" their time on poetry. Fortunately, in every class there are a few students who are interested in, if not excited by, poetry. They will have to suffice.

But on second thought: it really isn't enough. Not enough to justify a whole career of thirty-three years of teaching. No wonder so many young teachers don't last five years in today's classroom.

I'm sounding like Henri: I need affirmation for what I do in the classroom. And there is none. But there's nothing I can do about it except to go on pitching to these kids and hope something I say takes root in their minds and souls.

I tell my students that the literature they are reading now will help them live their lives. They look at me as if I were a creature from another planet. Of course, I can't go too deeply into the spirituality of literature in a public school. When I recently remarked to a colleague that our school fails to address the whole person, she nodded as if she were in complete agreement. I was surprised for she is well-known for her liberal political views, and I was expressing a rather conservative one.

I came across this and I thought both of my students and Father Nouwen:

> All works of art, whatever their content, have a spiritual dimension. They can be a source of strength and

75

consolation at times of difficulty. An ordinand I knew lost his faith in a way that left him desolate. He got through many difficult months by a sustained reading of Shakespeare. This was not just as a distraction from his pain; rather, what he read in Shakespeare reflected and gave depth to his own feelings about life at that time: its anguish and tragedy, delight and humour, its pointlessness and grandeur.[64]

I often feel rejected by my students. The antidote to this feeling, Nouwen says, is love. He writes: "When we truly love God and share in his glory, our relationships lose their compulsive character. We reach out to people not just to receive their affirmation, but also to allow them to participate in the love we have come to know through."[65]

As I come closer to the retreat, I've written an outline of some of the more important things I must say about Nouwen. In the Merton manner, Nouwen didn't offer his readers a manual of spiritual techniques. Retreatants should keep in mind the following:

1. Nouwen opens his heart to all those who wish to know God.
2. Nouwen leads his readers to God through his love of Jesus.
3. Nouwen advises his readers to carry their woundedness in imitation of Christ carrying his own cross.
4. Nouwen, like Merton, advises his readers to make

room for silence in their lives. Only then will they hear the "still, small voice."

5. Nouwen, like Merton, invites his readers to a deeper union with Christ. His invitation is couched in language that is simple but also eloquent.

If Nouwen has a spiritual discipline, it is a surrendering to Jesus. That is why the celebration of the Eucharist was so important to him.

Nouwen says: "Jesus has to be and to become ever more the center of my life. It is not enough that Jesus is my teacher, my guide, my source of inspiration. It is not even enough that he is my companion on the journey, my friend and my brother. Jesus must become the heart of my heart, the fire of my life, the love of my soul, the bridegroom of my spirit. He must become my only thought, my only concern, my only desire."[66]

At the end of his Genesee diary, Nouwen summarizes what the goal of his spiritual life entails:

> When I was a child, my mother taught me the simple prayer, "All for you, dear Jesus." A simple prayer indeed but hard to realize. I discovered that, in fact, my life was more like the prayer: "Let us share things, Jesus, some for you and some for me." The commitment to serve the Lord and him alone is hard to fulfill. Still, that is the mark of sanctity. My life has always been sort of a compromise. "Sure, I am a priest, but if they don't like me as a priest, then I can still show them that I am also a psychologist, and they

might like me for that." This attitude is like having hobbies on the side which offer gratification when the main task does not satisfy. The last seven months have revealed to me how demanding the love of the Lord is. I will never be happy unless I am totally, unconditionally committed to him. To be single-minded, to "will one thing," that is my goal and desire. Then also I can let go of the many pains and confusions that are the result of a divided mind. By allowing the Lord to be in the center, life becomes simpler, more unified, and more focused.[67]

Nouwen says we know ourselves for who we really are when we understand that we are sacred beings embraced by a loving God.

To acknowledge the truth of ourselves is to claim the sacredness of our being without truly understanding it. Our deepest being escapes our own mental or emotional grasp. But when we trust that our souls are embraced by a loving God, we can befriend ourselves and reach out to others in loving relationships.[68]

Nouwen learned from Merton the importance of solitude in the spiritual life. Some of his observations about solitude are:

I am becoming more and more aware that solitude indeed makes you more sensitive to the good in people and even enables you to bring it to the foreground.[69]

Solitude is a place where we can connect with profound bonds that are deeper than the emergency bonds of fear and anger. Although fear and anger indeed drive us together, they do not give rise to our love for one another. In solitude we come to the realization that we are not driven together but brought together.[70]

Solitude keeps us in touch with the sustaining love from which we draw strength. It sets us free from the compulsions of fear and anger and allows us to be in the midst of an anxious and violent world as a sign of hope and a source of courage.[71]

Retreatants should know Henri's three dominant goals: Home, Perfect Friend, and Unconditional Love.

Henri always grappled with the meaning of life. The following are a few of his observations,

To live a disciplined life is to live in such a way that you want only to be where God is with you. The more deeply you live your spiritual life, the easier it will be to discern the difference between living with God and living without God, and the easier it will be to move away from the places where God is no longer with you.[72]

Dare to love and to be a real friend. The love you give and receive is a reality that will lead you closer and closer to God as well as to those whom God has given you to love.[73]

Forgiveness is allowing other people not to be God.... Forgiveness requires letting go of hurts and disappointments and realizing that only God is capable of loving fully. It is futile to expect others to fulfill his role.[74]

Nouwen's spiritual way is one irradiated by beauty—beauty of act, beauty of word, beauty of thought, beauty of seeing and hearing. He followed beauty all his life. And he fell in love with beautiful things, like the icons he viewed and his own commissioned icons. He fell in love with Rembrandt's paintings. He fell in love with people: the beauty of their souls. Augustine says, "Do we love anything except what is beautiful?"[75]

I have followed beauty, primarily the beauty of literature. But like Nouwen, I am drawn to the visual arts and to music. But I have to admit I've never thought deeply about beauty's role in my spiritual life, and lately I find myself purchasing books on the theme of beauty. Some of the books I've acquired are *Saving Beauty* by Cardinal Martini; *Enjoying Beauty* by John Navone; *Art and the Beauty of God* by Richard Harries; *Toward a Theology of Beauty* by John Navone. The following passage helps me to understand the role of beauty in our inner lives:

> True beauty as attractiveness of the truly good motivates human life and development in that intellectual, moral, and religious self-transcendence that constitutes human authenticity. Without their attractiveness of beauty, intellectual, moral, and religious goods are bereft of their power to transform human life. Beauty is the enabling power of the truly good to draw us out of ourselves for the achievement of excellence.

> We cannot live without beauty. Our need for beauty
> is felt in the most basic demands of the human mind
> and heart.[76]

Back from a quick trip to New York City. This time I traveled by train. I visited the Frick Museum and stood for a long time before Bellini's *St. Francis in Ecstasy*. I tried to look upon this painting the way Nouwen would have, and then back on the train home I wrote the following:

I gazed upon this painting for over a half hour. So long I made the nearby attendant uneasy. But I was lost in attention, attempting to absorb the holy beauty of this portrait. To lessen her concern, I asked her what she thought of the painting. She answered me in a heavy Hispanic accent, "It's my favorite painting in the whole place." She also warned me not to forget the animals, "St. Francis loves animals." I found it interesting that she used the present tense: for her St. Francis lives in the Eternal Now. I returned to the painting to make sure I'd seen all the animals: the donkey (Brother Ass), the heron, the bird, the sheep. But to my surprise I'd not seen the rabbit emerging from the rocks. Of course, all these animals are emblematic and someday perhaps I'll have the time to consider more deeply their significance. I also noticed the naturalistic details of the painting: the beauty of the trees, flowers, rocks, blue sky and blue-tinted rocks. For St. Francis, similarly with the poet Hopkins, "The world is charged with the grandeur of God." From observing this painting, I understood more deeply the well known Franciscan joy in creation. I also noticed that St. Francis is barefoot, his sandals left at the entrance of his cave-cell, reminding me of the Transfiguration. There is also a lectern on which lies his Bible, above which hang a bell and rope likely used to announce the canonical hours. Here on Mount Alverna is all that is necessary for the life of the hermit. Of course, placed on the lectern is the human skull, the memento mori present throughout the history of Christian art, a reminder that we all must die one day.

I think of my life. I cannot be a hermit; I'm not a mystic; I'm not a saint. I'm standing in a museum that was formerly the home of an incredibly wealthy man, one requiring $9 million per year to operate. I also know that across the street in Central Park live many homeless people, mendicants like St. Francis and his friars. I had today already observed the ubiquitous panhandlers on the streets of New York City. The juxtaposition of wealth and poverty in New York is astonishing. I saw a panhandler standing on a corner before a Porsche and a woman impeccably dressed by haute couture swiftly passing a bag lady.

I know if St. Francis were alive, he'd be in Central Park seeking out the sick, the homeless, the drug addicts, the criminals. The man who kissed a leper would certainly reach out to touch the many afflicted with AIDS who sit on the ground with signs, "Please, I'm dying of AIDS." He would see God not only in every person he met but also in the natural beauty of the park created by Frederick Olmsted. He would be familiar with the birds, the labyrinthine paths, the flowers, the trees, and the small lakes. He'd also know the secret places where the insane hide themselves. In Living Room twelve there are other masterpieces, but St. Francis's radiance captures me totally; it almost seems that El Greco's St. Jerome on the opposite wall has also fixed his gaze on St. Francis.

My time spent with this painting is similar to prayer. After gazing upon Fra Angelico's Temptation of St. Anthony at the Metropolitan, Thomas Merton wrote, "Looking at this picture is exactly the same sort of thing as praying." What he meant is that in order to see one must forget the ego; by forgetting ourselves we are enabled to offer our complete attention to *what is before us and if it is beauty we're viewing, then God may touch us, for he is, as St. Augustine reminds us, the source of all beauty.*

I owe Nouwen and Weil and Rilke and Sister Wendy and Merton (and let me not forget Krishnamurti): They've helped me to see.

It's the day before the retreat. I'm anxious, of course. Today I'm outlining those passages from Nouwen that I believe are pivotal and need to be read aloud. Most of these come from three books: *Genesee Diary, The Return of the Prodigal Son,* and *Sabbatical Journey.*

Twenty-five people have registered for the retreat. Most of them are women. My friend, artist Anthony Lobosco, who has illustrated three of my books, has agreed to attend and take photographs of the day's proceedings. I hope *Walking with Henri Nouwen* will include photos of the retreatants and the beautiful interior of the main parlor, as well as the lovely grounds of St. Stephen Priory.

I'm glad I had the main parlor. I love its beamed ceiling and French doors and its old world decor. The room was crowded with over thirty people, many of them nuns living at the priory in a renewal program. There was a good number of people from my Merton Chapter, faces I've known for years. I began with Nouwen in the morning and concluded with Merton in the afternoon. The day flew by.

At the end of the second session, a nun came up to me and thanked me profusely. I was a little embarrassed. But she was sincere.

The nuns were great! They fully participated and their remarks and questions added energy to the day. I am glad I brought the enlarged copy of Rembrandt's painting; it elicited a deep discussion not only about the beauty of the art but about why it meant so much to Nouwen. We also gained a deeper understanding of Nouwen's desire for love and affection.

The nuns had no problem with either of the moral issues presented today: Merton's affair with his nurse and Nouwen's homosexuality. No problem because Merton didn't run off with M but remained a monk of Gethsemani. No problem with Nouwen because he didn't live with another man but remained faithful to his vocation and to celibacy.

Yet there was one man among the group who said that if a parish priest had been caught running around with his nurse, he would've been severely disciplined. Another person said to me that Nouwen would never have been accepted into a seminary if it were known he was a gay man. And that goes for today's seminaries too, she added. She wasn't angry, just commenting on the way it is. I said, "And what a loss that would've been for the world." She lowered her eyes and then looked into mine. "Yes, a great loss." And she meant it.

But what if Merton had married M? And what if Nouwen had come out of the closet? Would they have retained their positions as spiritual masters?

When I read the passages from Merton's *Learning to Love* journal, there was utter silence in the room. Many hadn't known about his falling in love with his nurse. Even I, as I read aloud the passages about his love for M, hadn't realized how head over heels in love he truly was. My speaking his own words aloud brought it home to me much more than previous silent readings. And the retreatants were very respectful of what he was undergoing; they empathized with his conflict and his pain.

They were impressed by Merton's love poems. Our Merton Chapter chairman came up to me and asked if he could borrow Merton's *Eighteen Poems.* "Bob, I'll guard it with my life. I'll just make copies of the poems." He knows how valuable the book is (250 copies were printed; I own copy 208); of course, I agreed.

I left all my Nouwen books on a round mahogany table near the podium. When the retreatants went to lunch, I saw a young woman going through them. She was from the West Coast.

"There are so many books, I don't know where to start."

"I suggest you start with his journals. Or with the *Return of the Prodigal Son.*"

"His life wasn't easy, was it?"

"No, but he managed pretty well considering the cards he was dealt."

"You mean about being a homosexual?"

"Yes, that among other things."

"It really doesn't matter in the end, does it?"

"Being a homosexual?"

"Yes. When you come right down to it, he only wanted what we all want, to love and to be loved."

"Yes, that's what it all comes down to."

I left her to her perusing. The book she held in her hand was Nouwen's *The Return of the Prodigal Son.*

After all my walking with Nouwen, is there any piercing insight that has helped me understand the man better?

Well, it recently occurred to me that I've *walked* with many writers both secular and religious. Merton and Nouwen, of course, have exerted a tremendous influence. But when I tried to zero in on whom Nouwen walked with during his life, I find one ever-present companion: Jesus Christ. Jesus was the center of Father Nouwen's life. I think that says it all. And it greatly colors how I now see the man.

Henri Nouwen is a role model for all men and women who are conflicted, who are wounded, who daily beat the hell out of themselves because they don't measure up to some impossible standard planted in their souls at an early age. Nouwen embraced his crosses, carried them, and allowed them to lead him to Jesus. And that, I believe, is what we all should try to emulate. There are some things about our personalities that won't change no matter how much we will it or how much therapy we seek. Then, it is best to surrender ourselves to Jesus, all that which is in the light and that which is in the shadow. Hand it all over to the One who is the Light of the world.

In such manner, we will be able to live our lives and fulfill our destiny.

Comments from Retreatants

❧ ❧

I forgot to provide a questionnaire at the end of the retreat. Just as they were leaving, I asked them if they could write a line or two about their day's experience. Here are a few.

The day was wonderful. It brought both Nouwen and Merton to Earth. I learned something about God, myself, and the two men.

I did not know anything about Nouwen. Now I think I will pick up one of his books. I knew very little about Merton and I was intrigued by his love affair with his nurse. But I am glad he remained a monk.

Thank you for today's journey and for throwing light on Merton's and Nouwen's journeys. Their inner struggles beautifully reveal the universal struggle that leads to transformed lives.

Nouwen's early childhood and the deprivation of touch deeply affected me. His writings *touch* the hearts of many because he has grown and matured through his woundedness.

The story of the Prodigal Son will never be the same for me. Thank you!

I had read almost nothing of Nouwen before the retreat, but I am now very interested in reading a great deal. What most strongly impressed me today was the work he did with the Prodigal Son and Rembrandt's painting. I had an epiphanic moment when Bob read Sister Wendy's description of the older son as so stiff and straight, and I realized that the father figure, rounded, enfolding, forgiving, was like a mother. I was also very moved by Nouwen's statement that forgiveness allows other people *not* to be God—and by his remarks about the creative journey embracing failure and leading to fuller self-understanding.

I found more than one answer today as I learned more about Thomas Merton and Henri Nouwen. My life will be different.

The fact that this great man, Henri Nouwen, found a home in helping handicapped people is an inspiration. Thomas Merton has always been an inspiration to me—the fact that he loved so deeply, so humanly, and yet remained faithful to God is beautiful.

This retreat about Nouwen and Merton has so impressed me that I realize the very heart of the day is the wonder of God and the strong faith of both men. They weren't perfect men, flawed pretty obviously. But also obvious is their love for God.

Because of Nouwen and Merton I want to know Christ. I want to feel as close to him as they did. Thank you.

Nouwen's frank admission of his woundedness has inspired me to face my own wound, one I've ignored for too long. I hope I can keep my resolve. Thank you for a beautiful day.

It was useful to examine the ways in which two different men possessed many talents and both wanted to discover how God called them to spend their lives in search of enlightenment. In spite of their intelligence and ability to use words effectively, both struggled with emotional issues as much as we simpler mortals do.

A Letter to Henri Nouwen

～～

In my book *Walking with Thomas Merton*, I wrote a letter to Merton thanking him for all his inspiration. I want to do the same with Father Nouwen.

Dear Father Nouwen,

I vividly remember you preaching at St. Paul's Church in Cambridge, Massachusetts. Your strong voice and your large, expressive hands made a deep impression on me, as well as your spiritual message of God's love for each of us.

Shortly after that night, I saw you in a local bookstore, and I wanted to go up to you and introduce myself. But my shyness won out, and my fear that I would be invading your privacy. But now that I understand you better through your journals and books, I know you would've welcomed my introduction. Perhaps we might've become friends. But I am your friend through your books. I greatly admire the utter honesty of your journals where you share so much of yourself with your readers. You are more intimate, more vulnerable than Merton was in his journals. I especially appreciate your candid descriptions of your woundedness.

I identify with your need for love and affection. As a teacher of literature, I often feel alienated from my students, the same way you felt about your students at Harvard. You offered them the gospel, which was often rejected. I offer my students Shakespeare and poetry, which they often reject or even hold in disdain. What speaks to my soul says nothing to them. But like you, I still try to reach them—and will do so as long as I remain in teaching—another year perhaps.

I also identify with your struggle to pray. I'm glad to read that you too love the Jesus Prayer. It's the prayer that has become a part of my being. Like you, I am drawn to great art because I believe it can speak to us of God. Your beautifully described aesthetic/spiritual experiences with Rembrandt and Van Gogh and others have moved me to try to train my eye to see. A deep holy life is a matter of seeing with the physical and the spiritual eye.

You touched me with your love for the handicapped, especially your love for Adam. I work with kids at the other end of the spectrum: gifted students. As talented as they are, they too have their own singular problems. But essentially they aren't so different from the handicapped: they crave attention. Too often they don't receive attention from their too-busy parents or from their overworked teachers. With more than 150 students daily, I have little time for one-on-one student interactions. I read so many essays about their loneliness and fear, and grading their essays seems sacrilegious.

You knew about loneliness and fear. You gazed upon the abyss. And you returned to everyday life intact. You advised people to embrace their woundedness. I think this advice is your greatest gift to our generation—for us to accept our brokenness and allow it to "break" us into beauty. As heroes in the past boasted about their war wounds, we should accept our wounds, share them, speak about them because they are what make each of us unique. Wounds are like fingerprints—no two are like. They make us who we are. And if we accept them in the right spirit, they move us into love and compassion so that when we meet other wounded men and women, we won't be afraid to reach out to them.

I'm always amazed to meet people who don't know about you. So in my small way, I try to introduce as many people as possible to you and your work through retreats. That's my way of saying "thank you" for coming into my life. At today's retreat there were a few people, I must admit, who had never heard of you, but they left the priory excited about knowing you better. Someone even left with one of my books!

Speaking of books, I was recently asked to make a list of the ten books that changed my life. Two of them were written by you. You are indeed a Spiritual Master. I understand that you would smile at such a lofty description of yourself. So, I'll simply say that you are a man of God—that, I think, says everything.

Sincerely,
Bob Waldron

Epilogue

∽ ∽

"Absolutely unmixed attention is prayer."[77]
Simone Weil

When I first read Simone Weil's definition of prayer as "absolutely unmixed attention," I felt a shock of recognition which evolved into an insight that has never left me: attention is the sine qua non of the spiritual life. I had previously thought only a privileged few could enter the depths of the spiritual life, those adept in the pursuit of holiness. Ordinary people like myself could only stand on the shore and wet their feet, never daring to go more deeply. Attention, however, is available to everyone no matter what their station in life or their degree of education.

To pay attention is not as easy as it sounds. To give one's complete attention to anything requires effort and energy. Attention is far from passive; rather, it is the mustering of our whole being to focus on something *other*. Attention demands, therefore, that we forget ourselves by setting aside our ego.

Anytime we achieve selflessness, accomplished when we are truly attentive, we are open for contact between the soul and God. Simone Weil says this kind of openness often occurs when we contemplate beauty, which, she says, is a snare for the soul, set by God so that God may enter it. God's snares are everywhere: in nature, in the arts, in people, and in *Lectio Divina*. Thus to be snared is to be captured by God. We must, however, be willing to be caught by God's traps, and willingness is dependent upon the degree of our attention.

Our raison d'être, therefore, is to seek out God's snares and become their willing victims. For example, when Christ exhorts us to gaze upon the beauty of the lilies, he is offering us the opportunity to be egoless,

> Look how the lilies of the field grow: they neither work nor spin. But I tell you, even Solomon in all his glory wasn't arrayed like one of them. But if God so clothes the grass of the fields, which is here today and thrown into the oven tomorrow, won't He clothe you much better, O you of little faith? (Matt 6:28–30)[78]

Implicit in beholding the beauty of the lilies is Christ's wisdom that to attain serenity we must learn to shift our attention from ourselves (egolessness) to something *other*. By offering our attention to beauty, we in effect offer it to God since God is the source of all beauty. In addition to beholding the beauty of the lilies, Christ exhorts us to "consider how they grow." This second imperative would require a lifetime of attention to exhaust its meaning; its attentive consideration is truly prayer.

But how many people are indeed willing to forget themselves? An epidemic of inattention has spread across our nation. The loss of the art of attention to details may have influenced today's national and international crises. On the spiritual level, inattention is the greatest hurdle for those who wish to develop a prayer life. Focusing on reading the New Testament or the Psalms is problematic for many people. In fact, those who intend to say morning and evening prayers often fail because they themselves are not attentive, succumbing too easily to the demands of the ego. Even attending Mass becomes perfunctory, just another duty inattentively fulfilled. And I am referring to ordinary people, not those who suffer from ADD: Attention Deficit Disorder.

How then can we develop our powers of attention so that we can pray without ceasing like the mystic Brother Lawrence who found God even among the pots and pans of his monastic kitchen? I believe it is a matter of will and desire. Weil states:

> Love is the teacher of gods and men, for no one learns without desiring to learn. Truth is sought not because it is truth but because it is good. Attention is bound up with desire. Not with the will but with desire—or more exactly, consent.
>
> We liberate energy in ourselves, but it constantly reattaches itself. How are we to liberate it entirely? We have to desire that it should be done in us—to desire it truly—simply to desire it, not to try to accomplish it. For every attempt in that direction is vain and has to be dearly paid for. In such a work all that I call "I" has to be passive. Attention alone—that attention which is so full that the "I" disappears—is required of me. I have to deprive all that I call "I" of the light of my attention and turn it on to that which cannot be conceived.[79]

In the act of contemplative awareness, we allow the desires of our ego to rest. We ourselves enter a space of silence where in our emptiness we allow ourselves to be penetrated by something *other*. It is this self-emptying (cf. *kenosis*) that invites God himself to rest in our hearts. This act of attention requires no mental gymnastics: we gently direct our attention to our chosen object and then forget ourselves so that God takes over. For a moment we might touch the hem of Jesus; for a moment we ourselves might be touched by Jesus; for a moment we might reach the still point of the turning wheel. Our lives become transfigured.

Attention moves us into selflessness, beyond which lies love; the last movement is contemplation where the observer and the observed become one. Attention's movement, however, is across a crystal bridge whose fragility cannot withstand the burdensome weight of the ego.

Endnotes

❧ ❧

1. Michael Ford, *Wounded Prophet: A Portrait of Henri J. M. Nouwen* (New York: Doubleday, 1999), p. 73.

2. Thomas Merton, *The Sign of Jonas* (New York: Harcourt Brace, 1948).

3. Henri Nouwen, *Sabbatical Journey: The Diary of His Final Year* (New York: Crossroad Publishing Company, 1998), p. 360.

4. Ibid., p. 361.

5. Ibid.

6. Rainer Maria Rilke, *Everyman Library* (New York: Alfred Knopf, 1996), p. 32.

7. John Eudes Bamberger, "Thomas Merton and Henri Nouwen: Living with God in Modern America," *Merton Seasonal: A Quarterly Review*, Summer 2000, p. 31.

8. Henri Nouwen, *Spiritual Journals* (New York: Continuum, 1998), p. 33.

9. Deirdre LaNoue, *The Spiritual Legacy of Henri Nouwen* (New York: Continuum, 2000), p. 14.

10. Henri Nouwen, *The Return of the Prodigal Son: A Story of Homecoming* (New York: Image Books, 1994), p. 33.

11. T. S. Eliot, *Murder in the Cathedral* (New York: Harcourt Brace & Company, 1935), p. 69.

12. *The Return of the Prodigal Son*, p. 100.

13. *Spiritual Journals,* p. 71.

14. Ibid., p. 32.

15. Ibid., p. 21.

16. *Spiritual Journals,* p. 312.

17. Ibid., p. 313.

18. Ibid., p. 378.

19. Ibid.

20. *Spiritual Journals,* p. 76.

21. *Sabbatical Journey,* p. 24.

22. Ibid., p. 25.

23. Ibid., pp. 318–19.

24. Ibid., p. 315.

25. Ibid., p. 363.

26. George A. Panichas (ed.) *The Simone Weil Reader: A Legendary Spiritual Odyssey of Our Time* (New York: David McKay Company, Inc., 1977), p. 474.

27. *Sabbatical Journey,* p. 105.

28. Jurjen Beumer, *Henri Nouwen: A Restless Seeking for God* (New York: Crossroad Publishing Company, 1997), p. 67.

29. *Sabbatical Journey,* p. 13.

30. Ibid., p. 39.

31. Ibid., p. 24.

32. *Wounded Healer,* p. 89.

33. Henri Nouwen, *Clowning in Rome* (New York: Doubleday, 2000), p. 100.

34. Beth Porter, editor, with Susan M. S. Brown and Philip Coulter, *Befriending Life: Encounters with Henri Nouwen* (New York: Doubleday, 2001), p. 262.

35. Henri Nouwen, *Letters to Marc about Jesus* (San Francisco: HarperSanFrancisco, 1988), p. 75.

36. Jose Maria Faerna, general editor, *Rouault* (New York: Cameo/Abrams, 1996), p. 18.

37. *Clowning in Rome*, p. 3.

38. Robert Lax, *Love Had a Compass: Journals and Poetry* (New York: Grove Press, 1996), pp. 60–62.

39. Ibid.

40. *Sabbatical Journey*, p. 39.

41. Ibid., p. 61.

42. *Befriending Life*, p. 92.

43. T. S. Eliot, *Murder in the Cathedral: The Complete Poems and Plays* (New York: Harcourt, Brace, Jovanovich, 1980), p. 196.

44. *Befriending Life*, p. 43.

45. Henri Nouwen, *The Inner Voice of Love: A Journey Through Anguish to Freedom* (New York: Doubleday, 1996), p. 3.

46. Ibid., p. 12.

47. *The New Testament, St. Paul Edition*, Mark A. Wauck, translator (Boston: Daughters of St. Paul, 2000) pp. 32–53.

48. *Inner Voice of Love*, p. 26.

49. Etty Hillesum, *An Interrupted Life* (New York: Henry Holt & Company, 1996), p. 55.

50. Ibid.

51. Henri Nouwen, *Reaching Out: The Three Movements of the Spiritual Life* (New York: Doubleday, 1986), p. 25.

52. *The Essential Herbert*, selected by Anthony Hecht (New York: Ecco Press, 1987), pp, 161–62.

53. *Spiritual Legacy of Henri Nouwen*, p. 84.

54. *Spiritual Journals*, p. 76.

55. Henri Nouwen, *Here and Now: Living in the Spirit* (New York: Crossroad Publishing Company, 1994), p. 105.

56. *Spiritual Legacy of Henri Nouwen*, p. 151.

57. *Inner Voice of Love*, p. 5

58. Paul Tillich, *The Shaking of the Foundations* (New York: Charles Scribner's Sons, 1948), p. 153.

59. *Sabbatical Journey*, p. 346.

60. Ibid., p. 388.

61. *Psychological Reflections*, editors: Jolande Jacobi and R.F.C. Hull (Princeton: Bollingen Paperback, 1973), p. 239.

62. Wallace Stevens, *The Palm at the End of the Mind*, edited by Holly Stevens (New York: Alfred Knopf, 1971), p. 7.

63. Dr. Edward Gray, *Discovering the Center* (New York/Mahwah, N.J.: Paulist Press, 2004).

64. Richard Harries, *Art and the Beauty of God* (London: Mowbray, 1993), p. 101.

65. *Sabbatical Journey*, p. 341.

66. Henri Nouwen, *Jesus and Mary: Finding Our Sacred Center* (Cincinnati: St. Anthony Messenger, 1993), p. 30.

67. *Spiritual Journals*, p. 130

68. Henri Nouwen, *Bread for the Journey: A Daybook of Wisdom and Faith* (San Francisco: HarperSanFrancisco, 1997), the entry for March 21.

69. *Spiritual Journals*, p. 71.

70. *Clowning in Rome*, p. 12.

71. Ibid., p. 14.

72. *Inner Voice of Love*, p. 23.

73. Ibid., p. 81.

74. "Moving from Solitude to Community to Ministry," *Leadership* (Spring 1995), p. 85.

75. Augustine of Hippo, *Confessions of St. Augustine,* John K. Ryan, translator (New York: Image Book, 1960), p. 106.

76. John Navone, *Towards a Theology of Beauty* (Collegeville, Minn.: Liturgical Press, 1996), p. 25.

77. Simone Weil, *Simone Weil: An Anthology,* edited by Sîan Miles (New York: Grove Press, 1986), p. 212.

78. *The New Testament, St. Paul Edition,* p. 32.

79. *Simone Weil: An Anthology,* p. 213.

Primary Sources

❧❧

Nouwen, Henri, *Behold the Beauty of the Lord: Praying with Icons* (Notre Dame: Ave Maria Press, 1987).

Nouwen, Henri, *Bread for the Journey: A Daybook of Wisdom and Faith* (San Francisco: HarperSanFrancisco, 1997).

Nouwen, Henri, *Clowning in Rome* (New York: Doubleday, 2000).

Nouwen, Henri, *Here and Now: Living in the Spirit* (New York: Crossroad Publishing Company, 1994).

Nouwen, Henri, *The Inner Voice of Love: A Journey Through Anguish to Freedom* (New York: Doubleday, 1996).

Nouwen, Henri, *Making All Things New: An Invitation to the Spiritual Life* (New York: Harper & Row, 1981).

Nouwen, Henri, *Pray to Live: Thomas Merton: Contemplative Critic* (Notre Dame: Fides/Claretian, 1972).

Nouwen, Henri, *Reaching Out: The Three Movements of the Spiritual Life* (New York, Doubleday, 1986).

Nouwen, Henri, *The Return of the Prodigal Son: A Story of Homecoming* (New York: Image Books, 1992).

Nouwen, Henri, *Sabbatical Journey: The Diary of His Final Year* (New York: Crossroad Publishing Company, 1998).

Nouwen, Henri, *Spiritual Journals* (New York: Continuum, 1998).

Nouwen, Henri, *With Burning Hearts: A Meditation on the Eucharistic Life* (New York: Orbis Books, 1994).

Nouwen, Henri, *The Wounded Healer* (New York: Doubleday, 1979).

Biography

Beumer, Jurjen, *Henri Nouwen: A Restless Seeking for God* (New York: Crossroad Publishing Company, 1997).

Ford, Michael, *Wounded Prophet: A Portrait of Henri J. M. Nouwen* (New York: Doubleday, 1999).

Porter, Beth, editor, with Susan M. S. Brown and Philip Coulter, *Befriending Life: Encounters with Henri Nouwen* (New York: Doubleday, 2001).

Criticism

LaNoue, Deirdre, *The Spiritual Legacy of Henri Nouwen* (New York: Continuum, 2000).

Secondary Sources

Eliot, T. S., *Murder in the Cathedral: The Complete Poems and Plays* (New York: Harcourt, Brace, Jovanovich, 1980).

Faerna, Jose Maria, general editor, *Rouault* (New York: Cameo/Abrams 1996).

Harries, Richard, *Art and the Beauty of God* (London: Mowbray, 1993).

Kennedy, Eugene, *The Unhealed Wound: the Church and Human Sexuality* (New York: St. Martin's Press, 2001).

Lax, Robert, *Love Had a Compass: Journals and Poetry* (New York: Grove Press, 1996).

Navone, John, *Toward a Theology of Beauty* (Collegeville: Liturgical Press, 1996).

Rilke, Rainer Maria, *Everyman Library* (New York: Alfred Knopf, 1996).

Weil, Simone, *Simone Weil: An Anthology*, edited by Sîan Miles (New York: Grove Press, 1986).